An Introduction Challenging Topics For Young Muslims

BOOK 1

By Dr Abdul Qader Ismail

Edited by Dr Musharraf Hussain

Invitation Publishing

First Edition Published February 2021

INVITATION PUBLISHING

512-514 Berridge Road West

Nottingham

NG7 5JU

Distributed by INVITATION PUBLISHING

Tel: +44[0] 115 855 0961

E-mail: info@invitationpublishing.co.uk

Cataloguing-in-Publication Data is available from the British Library.

ISBN: 978-1902248882

*For my mother and the mother of my children -
our first, and most important teachers.*

Written by Dr Abdul Qader Ismail BMBCh (Oxon), MA
(Oxon), MRCPCH, under the spiritual guidance of Khwaja
Muhammad Ulfat Qadri Naqshbandi (Lahore, Pakistan), and
Pir Mohammad Tayyab Ur-Rahman Qadri (Qadria Trust, UK;
Bhera Shareef, Haripur, Pakistan).

My most heartfelt thanks to Mullah Adil Bader, Dr Syed
Mutaheer Ali, and Mrs Atheah Gsouma for their help in
writing, editing and proofreading this book. These individuals
consented for their inclusion in this acknowledgement,
however, this does not mean they agree entirely with all, or any,
of what is written in this book. Similarly, I have not acted upon
all their feedback and suggestions during the writing, editing
and proofreading process.

I would also like to thank Mr Atif Hussain for keeping me
involved during the editing and publishing process, and Dr
Musharraf Hussain for his continued encouragement and
support.

Contents

Foreword

Young people are at a critical stage between childhood and adulthood. They are thinking on a higher level than children, but not yet confident in their view of the world like adults. Whilst children think logically about the concrete, the here and now, young people can think in abstract terms, about God, the life Hereafter and global concepts like the climate crisis. They have a heightened sense of justice, politics and patriotism. If they are not guided, they can develop unIslamic views on these topics and even accept conspiracy theories and extremist views. That is why it is so important that we guide young people. Dr Abdul Qader Ismail is to be congratulated on writing 'An Introduction to Challenging Topics for Young Muslims'. This book is a comprehensive manual for young people. He tackles subjects from belief in Allah to blood donation; from Riba to racism; and gambling to gender. He has based his book entirely on teachings of the Quran and the Sunnah of the blessed Messenger (peace be upon him). He has been thorough in ensuring that these sensitive matters are presented in a logical and effective style.

As young people wrestle with socio-religious, moral and spiritual perspectives it is important to provide them clear guidelines, set boundaries of dos and don'ts; give them confidence that they are special and they have not been left alone to wonder in the wilderness of a largely secular and sometimes aggressively atheist society. Nor are they left at the mercy of social media platforms to inform themselves of such important issues.

Dr Abdul Qader Ismail is a young paediatrician trained at Oxford University. His passion to educate his family and the Muslim youth is to be much-admired. I pray Allah give him more energy, time and resources to continue doing this kind of educational work.

Dr Musharraf Hussain Al-Azhari

(Translator of 'The Majestic Quran')

Introduction

The topics introduced in this book include:

- Philosophical and theological questions, such as why do we believe in God, why there are so many different religions, why there are so many sects in Islam?

- Some common objections raised against Islam, e.g. validity of the Qur'an and Hadith, apparent contradictions between Islam and science, and Hudud punishments in the Shariah.

- Current issues regarding relationships and gender identity, vegetarianism and environmentalism.

- Behavioural, physical and mental health issues, e.g. coping with the stress of exams, obesity, anxiety and depression, self-harm and suicide.

- Addictive habits e.g. drugs, alcohol and smoking, gambling, and watching pornography.

These are all important socioreligious topics which are introduced in school, by friends, or on the internet. The information we gain from these sources may not be accurate, will very likely be secular, or worse, have an Islamophobic agenda. This can have very damaging consequences; it can create serious doubt in our minds regarding our faith especially when we have not yet developed a strong, personal relationship with it.

Parents and Islamic school teachers should be involved when using this book as a guide to navigate these topics so that you can develop a strong foundation and a firm understanding of your faith. You will realise how Allah and His Prophet (peace be upon him), in the Qur'an and Hadith, and through the interpretation of Islamic scholars in every age, have provided us with important principles and guidance which are as relevant today as they were over 1400 years ago. This is an ongoing process as the world, society and science evolve, so too does our understanding of our faith. This will better prepare you for the secular and sometimes hostile environment encountered in schools, in the media and on the internet.

1. ISLAM, FROM ANCIENT TIMES TO THE MODERN DAY

1 . 1

Believing in Allah

Objectives

- To understand what faith is

- To explore the different arguments put forward for the existence of God

- To consider what proof you, as a Muslim have for your belief in Allah

Keywords

- Faith

- Belief

- Atheism

- Theism

The beliefs of a Muslim are based on the teachings of the Prophet Muhammad, and what is contained within the Revelation he was sent with, the Qur'an. But to believe in the Prophethood of Muhammad (peace be upon him) and the Qur'an as Revelation, we must first believe in the existence of Allah. Why do we believe this? Especially in the modern, scientific world we live in, does it make sense to believe in God? Can we prove that Allah exists?

What is faith?

One definition of faith is to have a strong belief, in the absence of evidence. In the Qur'an, this is called believing in the 'unseen' (Ghayb).

This is the Majestic book, there is no doubt in it, a guidance for the pious, who believe in the unseen, perform prayer and spend in charity from what We have provided them. They believe in what is revealed to you and what was revealed before you, and they have firm faith in the Hereafter. (Qur'an 2:2-4)

He is the Knower of the unseen and doesn't reveal His secrets to anyone, except the Messengers of His choosing... (Qur'an 72:26-27)

In fact, this is part of its value, that it is 'unseen' (that it cannot be proven by using scientific methods used to study the world around us), and yet we believe it in.

If there was undeniable scientific evidence (such as there being oxygen in the air we breathe, or the presence of a blackhole at the centre of our galaxy), then it would no longer be called 'believing' or 'having faith', as everyone would accept it as fact. This is not to say that there isn't any evidence for the existence of Allah, but that it won't be the same kind of evidence for physical things. The only time a non-believer will have hard evidence is at the time of death when they come to see the Angel of death and Allah's punishment. Though they now have proof, their repentance at this stage is not accepted.

There is no repentance for those who keep on doing evil deeds until death approaches them, then say: "Now I repent," nor for those who die as disbelievers. For such We've prepared a painful punishment. (Qur'an 4:18)

So when they saw Our punishment they declared, "We believe in Allah; the One and we reject any partner we associated with Him." Their belief won't benefit them now, since they have seen our punishment. This was the way of Allah among His servants in the past, the disbelievers will be utter losers there. (Qur'an 40:84-85)

The Prophet (peace be upon him) said: "Allah will accept the repentance of His slave so long as the death-rattle has not yet reached his throat." (Tirmidhi)

Therefore, we do not have, and are not meant to have absolute scientific proof that Allah exists (but as we will discuss later on, this is not to say there is no evidence at all that points towards the existence of God).

Atheism

Atheism is the belief that God does not exist as opposed to theism, the belief that God does exist. Since it is impossible to prove or disprove the existence of God, it could be argued that both theists and atheists have faith (i.e. a strong belief in something in the absence of evidence). It could also be argued that a true scientist would be an agnostic, neither believing that God exists nor doesn't exist due to lack of evidence one way or the other.

Some people wrongly believe that all scientists are atheists, and people who believe in science cannot believe in God. While it is true that many scientists are atheists (famous examples including Richard Dawkins and Stephen Hawking), there are also many who do believe in a God or Higher Being, or are agnostic and say that as scientists, we cannot definitely say God does not exist. Famous examples include Isaac Newton, Albert Einstein, Charles Darwin, Marie Curie, Blaise Pascal, Gregor Mendel, Louis Pasteur, Max Planck, etc.

However, while agnosticism might be a starting position on this debate, it shouldn't be the final destination. Believing in the existence of God changes everything about the way we live our life and how we view the world around us, therefore it is important to take this question seriously and arrive at a conclusion one way or the other, with clear understanding of our thought process.

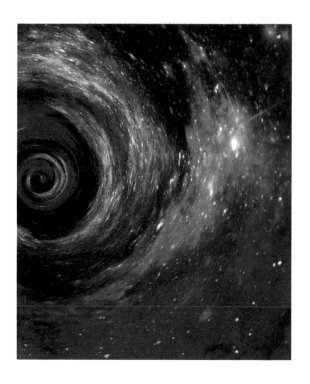

A decision that impacts on eternity

The Gambler's Argument (or Pascal's Wager) is based on the writings of the philosopher and mathematician Blaise Pascal. He sets out what an agnostic should do to maximise his chances of having a good outcome from life while minimising the risk of having a bad outcome. There are two possible courses of action leading to four possible outcomes:

1. He believes in God but turns out to be wrong. This will result in having wasted time and effort in this life worshipping an imaginary God, and not indulging in some worldly pleasures.

2. He believes in God and turns out to be right. This will result in gaining the reward of eternal life in Paradise.

3. He doesn't believe in God and turns out to be right. This will result in a life lived free to indulge in worldly pleasures without guilt because there is no God to judge him.

4. He doesn't believe in God and turns out to be wrong. This will result in being punished for eternity in Hell.

Pascal argued that the most rational choice is to believe in God and live your life accordingly. That way, even if wrong, you wouldn't lose as much compared to what you gain if you are right. In contrast to this, it is irrational to disbelieve in God since what you gain even if you are right is insignificant compared to what you stand to lose if you are wrong.

While the conclusion of this argument, that we should believe in God just in case He exists, is not a solid foundation for faith, it does raise a very important question for atheists and agnostics. Have

they given this most important and fundamental question of whether God exists enough consideration? Have they ever really approached it with an open heart and mind, to feel content and willing to face the consequence of spending eternity in Hell if they are wrong?

When it was said: "Allah's promise is true and there is no doubt in the coming of the Final Hour," you replied, "We don't know what the Final Hour is; we assumed it's an idea, and we weren't convinced at all." The evil consequences of their deeds will become clear to them as they are overcome by what they mocked. They will be told: "Today We'll forget you as you forgot the meeting of this Day of yours; this is your destination – Hell. You have no helpers. That is because you mocked Allah's verses and were deceived by worldly life." So today they won't be taken out of it, nor given any opportunity to explain themselves. (Qur'an 45:32-35)

God of the gaps

The 'God of the gaps' argument says that in the past, when humans saw things that they did not understand or were not able to explain, they ascribed them to God. For example by believing that thunder was His speech and lightning was His weapon they used God to fill in the gaps in their understanding of the world around them.

Over time, as science and technology have advanced we have a much better understanding of the world we live in, and why things happen the way they do. We can now explain things people in previous ages were not able to, and so we no longer have to believe that they are due to God. In the same way, even if there are still many things about the world and Universe that we are still trying to understand, we can expect that future generations will be able to explain them due to further scientific advances. Therefore, there is no need to believe in God.

However, as Muslims we reject this argument because we do not believe in Allah to explain the gaps in our understanding of how the natural world works. In fact, the opposite is true. Again and again, Allah tells us in the Qur'an to do science, to study the world around us, to understand and think about how Allah has

created the Universe and the natural laws He made to govern it. Out of all of His creation, He has blessed humans with this ability. Therefore, as Muslims, the more our advancing science and technology allows us to understand the natural world, the more it increases our belief in Allah, rather than decreasing it.

He laid out the land with mountains and running rivers, produced fruits in pairs, and covered the day by the darkness of the night. Surely in this are signs for insightful people. There are neighbouring plots, vineyards, fields and palms, growing either in clusters or standing alone; all are fed by the same water, yet some are better to eat than others. Surely, in this are signs for people who understand. (Qur'an 13:3-4)

He created the night and the day for your benefit; the sun, the moon and the stars all follow His command. In that are signs for those who understand. He produced objects of many colours
on the Earth for you; in that are signs for those who accept advice. For your benefit He created the sea; from it you get fresh meat to eat, and extract jewellery that you wear. You see the ships sailing over the waves to seek His gifts, so you may be thankful. He placed the mountains firmly on the Earth, so it doesn't shake beneath you, made the rivers and the tracks so you can find your way, and many other signposts, including the stars for guiding the travellers. (Qur'an 16:12-16)

Answering the bigger questions

Science helps us understand how things happen, but it does not provide us with answers to the deeper questions, such as what is the purpose of life and what happens after we die. Allah has provided us with these answers through a different type of knowledge, that of Revelation sent to Prophets (peace be upon them all).

We revealed to you as We revealed to Nuh and the Prophets after him; and We revealed to Ibrahim, Ismail, Ishaq, Yaqub, the Tribes, Isa, Ayyub, Yunus, Harun and Sulayman; and We gave Dawud the Psalms. There were Messengers that We told you about, and there are other Messengers that We haven't told you about, and Allah spoke directly to Musa. There have been Messengers bearing both good news and warnings so that, after the Messengers, people would have no defence against Allah... (Qur'an 4:163-165)

...We revealed to you a glorious Book that explains the truth about all things; it is guidance, a kindness and good news for the Muslims. (Qur'an 16:89)

"People, your Lord's teachings have come to you; they're a healing balm for the diseases of the heart, and guidance and goodwill for the believers." (Qur'an 10:57)

I created Jinn and human beings only to worship Me. (Qur'an 51:56)

Do they not think that they will be resurrected unto a tremendous day – a day when mankind shall stand before the Lord of the worlds? (Qur'an 83:4-6)

On that Day, people will come forward in separate groups to be shown their deeds: whoever has done an atom's weight of good will see it, but whoever has done an atom's weight of evil will see that. (Qur'an 99:6-8)

Allah will say to the righteous, "O tranquil soul! Return to your Lord, well pleased [with Him] and well pleasing [to Him]. So join My servants, and enter My Paradise." (Qur'an 89:27-30)

Indeed, Hell has been lying in wait for the transgressors, a place of return, in which they will remain for ages [unending]. They will not taste therein any coolness or drink except scalding water and dirty wound discharges - an appropriate recompense [according to their evil acts]! (Qur'an 78:21-26)

So, through faith in God and religion we learn about our purpose in life and how to fulfil it, which will lead us to Paradise in the afterlife. Science alone cannot provide us with these answers.

Part of human nature

Countless human civilisations, from the first humans to the present day, from all parts of the world, with different cultures and languages, have all had belief systems that involve a Higher Being, a Creator, a God. This shows us that belief is part of the natural human state, like an instinct. In Islam this is called the Fitra – the natural state Allah created all humans with.

Remember when Your Lord took all the offspring from the loins of the children of Adam to be witnesses, saying, "Am I not your Lord?" They replied, "Yes, we bear witness." This was so that, on Judgement Day, you would not say, "We were unaware of this covenant" ... (Qur'an 7:172)

So set your face towards the religion of Allah with sincerity and adhere to people's nature which Allah shaped. There is no change in the laws of Allah's creation... (Qur'an 30:30)

This is further supported by the fact that when people face sudden, intense difficulties (such as a family death, or being attacked and fearing for their lives), many of those who would consider themselves non-religious or atheists will still call out to a Higher Being for help in their desperation. Again, Allah describes this within the Qur'an.

Ask them: "Who rescues you from the dark dangers of land and sea when you call Him humbly in secret for help, all the while thinking to yourselves, 'If He rescues us from this we will, indeed, be thankful'?" Say: "It is Allah Who rescues you from that and every other danger, but then you go back to associated false gods." (Qur'an 6:63-64)

In bad times people call on their Lord, longing for Him; when He treats them kindly, a group of them continues to associate partners with their Lord, being ungrateful for what We gave them... (Qur'an 30:33-34)

Rational belief

Philosophers and theologians have put forward many arguments for the existence of God. While none of them serve as proof, they do show that theism is a rational position. In this section I will provide a summary of the two most famous.

The unmoved Mover, the uncaused Cause, the uncreated Creator

Many famous philosophers and theologians put forward this theory in slightly different forms, including Aristotle, Imam Ghazali (may Allah have mercy upon him), and Thomas Aquinas. They said that whatever begins to exist must have a cause for its existence. The Universe began to exist at some point in time. Therefore, the Universe must have a cause.

This argument only works if at some point there must be an uncaused cause, otherwise there could exist an infinite cycle of cause and effect. If we accept this, then the uncaused cause must be different from everything else, it must be unique. Since it created the Universe, it must be outside of space and time and incredibly powerful. It would also be incredibly knowledgeable since it set up all the laws that govern the entire Universe. This uncaused Cause, or uncreated Creator matches the description of God.

Indeed, the most widely accepted theory for how the Universe began is the Big Bang. This describes how, about 13.8 billion years ago the Universe (all of space and time) went from smaller than an electron in size to nearly its current size within a fraction of a second. Islamic scholars believe Allah has told us of this event within the Qur'an.

Don't the disbelievers know the heavens and the Earth were joined at one time? We split them apart... (Qur'an 21:30)

An objection to the uncaused cause argument is that just because everything we study within the Universe has a beginning and therefore a cause, we cannot say the same about the Universe as a whole. Another objection is that the argument is based on an assumption that an infinite cycle of cause and effect is impossible, and so says there must be a first cause, giving it special properties to justify belief in God. Even if we accept this step of the argument, what is to say there must be just one uncaused Cause; why not two, ten, or even hundreds?

The teleological/ intelligent design argument

Imam Abu Hanifa (may Allah have mercy upon him) was once due to have a debate with an atheist. The Imam was several hours late. Upon arrival he explained that on his way he had come to the river Tigris and could not find a boat to cross. While waiting, he saw something astounding. Planks of wood that were floating nearby suddenly started coming together. Then some nails appeared and began to join the planks together. Water was leaking through the planks until some sort of sealant drifted down

the river and poured itself between the planks causing them to become watertight. All of a sudden, a sail appeared and he noticed that a boat had formed before his eyes. It travelled towards him and when he climbed on, it navigated safely across the river without him having to control it in anyway. This is the reason he was late. The atheist burst out laughing that Imam Abu Hanifa was caught telling such an obvious lie. The Imam turned to him and said, "If you cannot believe that a boat came into being without a boat maker, then this is only a boat, how can you believe that the whole world, the Universe, the stars, the oceans, and the planets came into being without a Creator?"

William Paley, a British Christian, put forward a similar argument called the Watchmaker Analogy. It basically says that if you came across a mechanical pocket watch while walking in the park, would you look at its complicated gears and springs that all fit together perfectly to allow it to tell the time so accurately and assume it had come about through natural processes or would you know that it must have been created by a watchmaker?

These are examples of the teleological, or intelligent design argument for the existence of God. In its most current form it uses the fact that the Universe is incredibly fine-tuned for the existence of life. According to physicist and philosopher Robin Collins, "If the initial explosion of the Big Bang had differed in strength as little as one part in 10^{60} (ten with 60 zeroes after it), the Universe would have either quickly collapsed back on itself, or expanded too rapidly for stars to form. In either case, life would be impossible." Renowned physicist Stephen Hawking estimates that, "If the rate of the Universe's expansion one second after the Big Bang had been smaller by even 1 part in 100,000,000,000,000,000, the Universe would have re-collapsed into a hot fireball due to gravitational attraction."

There are many other examples of this 'fine-tuning' including the strength of fundamental forces (e.g. gravity and electromagnetism), and the mass of electrons, protons and neutrons. Any one of these by itself would be a huge coincidence, but for so many of the basic laws of our Universe to be so exact, allowing life to exist, has led to the argument that the Universe must have been created or designed in such a way, for this purpose.

Indeed, Allah tells us this in the Qur'an, how He created the Universe for our use, to allow us to fulfil our purpose; to worship Him.

We honoured the children of Adam...and favoured them above all Our creation. (Qur'an 17:70)

For your benefit He created the sea; from it you get fresh meat to eat, and extract jewellery that you wear. You see the ships sailing over the waves to seek His gifts, so you may be thankful. He placed the mountains firmly on the Earth, so it doesn't shake beneath you, made the rivers and the tracks so you can find your way, and many other signposts, including the stars for guiding the travellers. (Qur'an 16:14-16)

Allah created the heavens and the Earth and sent down rain from the sky, by which He produced fruits to provide for you, and made possible for you to sail by ship across the sea by His command, made rivers for you, made the sun and the moon, orbiting steadily, and made for you both night and day. (Qur'an 14:32-33)

Both atheists and theists have several objections to the teleological / intelligent design argument. This is because it is arguing for a 'God of the gaps' to explain the complexity, diversity, and what seems like purpose in the natural world. But because of scientific advances we have a better understanding of how this has come about, e.g. the theory of evolution explains the amazingly complicated and sheer number of different life forms we share this planet with. According to the teleological argument, this would mean we do not need to believe in God.

Another theory put forward to explain this idea of fine-tuning is the concept of a Multiverse – an infinite collection of Universes including our own. Every Universe has different properties, and because they are infinite, all possibilities must exist within the Multiverse. Therefore, it is a necessity that in at least one of the Universes all the natural laws line up to be perfect for the existence of life. Because we are living in this Universe, and unaware of the infinite other Universes where life does not exist, we assume that our Universe is the only one and it has been fine-tuned to allow our existence, and that this means there must be a God. While the concept of a Multiverse is theoretically possible, there is no scientific evidence to support it.

Is there any evidence for the existence of God?

Miracles of the Prophets

In the Qur'an Allah describes several miracles He granted to His Prophets (peace be upon them all). For example, when the people of Thamud asked their Prophet Salih for a miracle, a mountain split apart and a giant she-camel emerged.

And to the people of Thamud We sent their brother Salih. He said, "O my people! Worship Allah—you have no other god except Him. A clear proof has come to you from your Lord: this is Allah's she-camel as a sign to you. (Qur'an 7:73)

When Nimrod threw the Prophet Ibrahim into the pyre, Allah commanded the fire to become cool so His Prophet wouldn't be harmed.

They said: "Burn him, and give victory to your gods if you will do anything." We said: "O fire, be cool and safe upon Abraham." (Qur'an 21:68-69)

Allah granted the Prophet Isa the ability to blow life into clay birds:

...and (We will make Jesus) a Messenger to the children of Israel (saying) that: 'I have come to you with a sign from your Lord. I will make for you from clay like a figure of a bird, breathe into it, and it will become a bird by the permission of Allah. (Qur'an 3:49)

Miracles are events that occur by the power and will of Allah, and contravene the natural laws that He created to govern His Universe. They can therefore appear as magic tricks and the Qur'an tells us how they are often labelled as such by people who refuse to believe in the message of their Prophet.

In the story of the Prophet Musa, magicians from all over Egypt were brought together to challenge him in front of the people, to show that his 'miracles' were nothing more than magic tricks. When the magicians witnessed what Musa was able to do they realised this was not magic and must be through the power of Allah, and so believed in him as a Prophet.

So he (Musa) threw his shepherd's staff, and straightaway it turned into a snake, everyone saw that;

next he pulled his hand out from his clothes, and it looked white to the onlookers. The leaders of Pharaoh's people said, "He's an expert magician, he wants to expel you from your land, so what do you suggest?" They said, "Delay him and his brother, in the meantime, send messengers to the cities to bring every experienced magician here." The Magicians came to the Pharaoh, they asked, "Will we be rewarded if we win?" He said, "Yes! You will join people who are in my inner circle." They said, "Musa, either you go first, or let us go first?" He said, "You start." So they went first, conjuring up a trickery for people's eyes to frighten them, and made an impressive magical spectacle. Then We urged Musa, "Throw down your staff," and at once it began to swallow up their fake devices. So the truth came out, and what they had been doing was shown to be

worthless. *They were defeated and made to look unimportant. The magicians threw themselves to the ground in prostration, saying: "We believe in the Lord of all the realms, the Lord of Musa and Harun." Pharaoh said, "How dare you believe before I give you permission! This is some cunning plot that you have all devised in this city to expel its people. You will soon know where true power lies. I will have your hands and feet cut off on the opposite sides and crucify you all." They said, "We hand ourselves over to our Lord. What reason do you have to take revenge on us except that we believed in the signs of our Lord when they came? Our Lord, give us patience, and let us die in submission to You." (Qur'an 7:107-126)*

Therefore, for the people who witness them and those who believe in them, miracles provide proof for the existence of God. Indeed, that is their purpose and why they were granted to Prophets.

Scientific facts within the Qur'an

Certain passages of the Qur'an have been interpreted in light of relatively modern scientific discoveries. I have mentioned some examples here. The Qur'an describes the light from the Sun and Moon differently, the Sun is described with words that mean it produces its own light, whereas the Moon is described with words that mean it reflects light.

Blessed is He Who placed constellations in the sky, and made brilliant stars, a shining sun and a bright moon. (Qur'an 25:61)

Regarding the Sun, Earth and Moon, the Arabic words used to describe their motion mean moving on a set path that involves coming back to their starting point, which we now interpret as their orbits.

He created night and day, sun and moon, each one moving in its orbit. (Qur'an 21:33)

On Earth, Allah describes the mountains as pegs, holding it steady, and we now know that mountains have roots that extend deep into the Earth, and they do act to stabilise the Earth.

We made the mountains on Earth for stability, so it does not shake beneath them... (Qur'an 21:31)

Allah describes how He made all life on Earth from water.

...and made every living thing from water; won't they believe? (Qur'an 21:30)

Within the womb of a mother, the Qur'an describes different stages of embryonic development, including how it attaches firmly to the wall of the uterus, before looking like a leech or blood clot, hanging from the wall of the uterus, filled with blood vessels, and then as a chewed lump of flesh, and how bones and muscles develop.

...We placed him as a drop of semen in the stable environment of the womb. The drop of semen turned to a bloodlike clot; and, from the bloodlike clot, We created a fleshy lump; and then We made bones and covered them with flesh; then We produce from it another created form. Blessed is Allah, the best Creator. (Qur'an 23:12-14)

Given that it would have been impossible for the Prophet Muhammad (peace be upon him)

to have been aware of such things over 1400 years ago, Muslims argue that this proves the Divine nature of the Qur'an and the Prophethood of Muhammad (peace be upon him). For a more in-depth discussion regarding science and the Qur'an, please read the chapter entitled 'Islam, Science, and the Theory of Evolution'.

The miracle of the Qur'an

The Qur'an is considered the greatest miracle Allah gave to the Prophet Muhammad (peace be upon him).

They said: "If only miracles were sent down to him from his Lord." Say: "Miracles come from Allah, and I am a clear warner." Isn't it enough that We revealed the

Book to you so it may be recited to them? … (Qur'an 29:50-51)

The Prophet (peace be upon him) said: "Every Prophet was given miracles on account of which their people believed; but I have been given Divine Revelation which Allah has revealed to me, and I am hopeful that my followers will outnumber the followers of other Prophets on Resurrection Day." (Bukhari)

Unlike the other miracles he was granted or the miracles given to previous Prophets (peace be upon them all), the Qur'an was not only for that time, place and people, but for all of humanity until the Day of Judgement. This is because he was the final Prophet and Messenger of Allah and the Qur'an was the final Revelation.

If we take it in its entirety, the Qur'an was revealed over a period of 23 years. The Prophet (who was illiterate and received no formal education) was reciting Qur'anic verses to his companions on a daily basis during this time. They memorised it and wrote it down, but he was not reading from a book he had previously written, nor was he spending his time preparing speeches for what to say to them.

Have you ever tried to deliver even a short, unprepared speech to an audience without reading it from a script? It is nearly impossible not to pause in places, to 'umm' and 'ahhh', to unintentionally say the wrong thing or in the wrong way and have to correct yourself, to contradict yourself, to forget what you were going to say and to later think that you could have said it in a much better way. What if you tried giving the same speech the next day, or in a week or months' time, without having it written down with you? Would you be able to recite it word for word identical to the original? Would you want to, or would you try to improve it and remove inconsistencies and mistakes you made saying it the first time? When we listen to politicians being interviewed by journalists, how many times are they questioned about something they said in the past with absolute conviction, yet now they find themselves having to backpedal and uncomfortably justify or correct?

Yet there are no reports of any of this occurring during the entire 23 years in which the Qur'an was revealed, recited and recorded by the companions of the Prophet (may Allah be pleased with them all). And consider that in its entirety, the Qur'an contains over 77,000 words, is so concise that each verse and the specific words it contains are essential to portraying its multiple meanings and underlying message. It is neither prose or poetry and is not structured like other books that have a start and an end, instead weaving its interconnected themes into each chapter and verse.

Some might argue that his companions would have covered it up. But the Prophet (peace be upon him) lived among his enemies for a significant part of these 23 years, reciting the Qur'an directly to them. Even his staunchest enemies, who refused to accept Islam out of pride and hatred towards the Prophet (peace be upon him), had to admit that they had heard nothing as eloquent and perfect as the Qur'an, despite the Arabs of the time being experts of language and poetry.

In fact, due to the profound effect of hearing it, the Prophet's enemies had to find ways to discourage people from listening to him at all. They did this through a smear campaign, telling people that he was a magician and would cast a spell on them and so to stay away from him and not engage him in conversation. They would follow him around and purposefully make noise during recitation of the Qur'an to not only stop themselves from hearing the beautiful words, but also anyone else. Yet they could not keep away themselves, and there are reports of them coming at night, in secret to listen to its recitation.

Is there any other speech in the history of mankind, given over nearly two and half decades, and so vast as to cover topics from the

Divine and the Devil, history of Prophethood and Revelation, the creation of the Universe and the end of times, natural phenomenon from insects to the cosmos, and humanity – as individuals and within society, yet not only doesn't contain any inconsistencies or contradictions but reveals scientific facts not discovered until hundreds of years later, and words of such perfection and beauty that even its staunchest enemies can't help themselves from wanting to listen to it? For over 1400 years scholars have spent their entire lives studying it, writing volumes upon volumes of books of commentary, yet don't claim to have uncovered all its secrets. Furthermore, it contains prophecies that have all come true to date, including the victory the Muslims in the battle of Badr, the conquest of Makkah, the victory of the Romans over the Persians, preservation of Pharaoh's body, protection of the Qur'an from being corrupted like previous Revelations, ease of memorisation of the Qur'an, etc.

All of this leads us to question how a human being, even if they were the most intelligent to have ever lived, would be able to accomplish this?

Your companion has neither strayed nor erred; nor does he speak from personal desire. It is a Divine inspiration. (Qur'an 53:2-4)

Muslims argue that those who study the Qur'an with an open heart and mind will necessarily conclude that it truly is of Divine origin. This is why Allah issues an unanswerable challenge to those who refute this, to come up with its like.

Say, "If all humanity and Jinn got together to bring a book like this Qur'an, they wouldn't be able to bring it, no matter how much they helped each other." (Qur'an 17:88)

And they say, "He has invented it?" Say: "Then fetch ten chapters like it that you have invented, and call as witnesses whomever you can besides Allah, if you are telling the truth. (Qur'an 11:13)

If you have doubts about what We have revealed to Our servant, then produce a chapter like it and call all your witnesses and supporters besides Allah; that is if you are truthful. If you have not done so – and you will never be able to do so – then fear the Fire whose fuel is people and brimstone, prepared for the disbelievers. (Qur'an 2:23-24)

Personal religious experience

Muslims who spend their time trying to worship Allah as best they can and who submit to His will develop a strong personal relationship with Allah. This takes many years, even decades to develop, and at times has its ups and downs as our level of faith increases and decreases based on what else is going in our life.

... A light from Allah has come to you, and a clear book, by this Allah guides anyone who follows the paths of peace in search of His pleasure, it takes them out of darkness into the light by His authority, and guides them on the straight path. (Qur'an 5:15-16)

Believers, be mindful of Allah and believe in His Messenger, so you are given a double share of His kindness. He will offer you a light to walk in, and forgiveness. Allah is the Forgiving, the Caring. (Qur'an 57:28)

...those who believe, their hearts will find peace in Allah's remembrance. The fact is, hearts find peace in the remembrance of Allah! (Qur'an 13:28)

Despite this, by remaining steadfast and continually putting in the effort

to nurture this most important relationship will bring a sense of peace and fulfilment in our lives and a certainty regarding the existence of Allah that doesn't need any further proof and eventually reaches a level where it cannot be shaken by life events. This is because we will develop an inner strength due to the absolute belief that everything that happens only happens by the will of Allah.

He has the keys of the unseen realm, only He knows them. He knows all that is in the land and the sea. Not a single leaf falls without His knowledge, no seed buried in the darkness of the earth, nor any fresh or withered plant is left unrecorded in a clear Book. (Qur'an 6:59)

"Any disaster on Earth or to yourselves is written down before it happens; this is easy for Allah." (Qur'an 57:22)

"If a calamity befalls you, do not say, 'If only I had done that, it would have been like that.' Say instead, 'It is the destiny of Allah and He does whatever He wishes' for surely 'if' opens the door for Shai'tan." (Muslim)

We will come to know that any difficulty we face will not be more than we can bear. In fact, it will contain some benefit for us and will eventually pass when we have patience and absolute trust and reliance on Allah. Indeed, this is the process by which He elevates our ranks, by which we can draw closer to Him.

"How wonderful is the affair of the believer, for his affairs are all good, and this applies to no one but the believer. If something good happens to him, he is thankful for it and that is good for him. If something bad happens to him, he bears it with patience and that is good for him." (Muslim)

"Whatever Allah has decreed for His believing slave is a blessing, even if that is in the form of withholding; it is a favour even if that is in the form of a trial; and the calamity decreed by Him is fair, even if it is painful." (Madaarij al-Saalikeen)

Indeed, every hardship is followed by ease, indeed, every hardship is followed by ease. (Qur'an 94:5-6)

Therefore, for the individual Muslim, the real proof for the existence of Allah is within their heart, born of the relationship they have developed with the Divine through years of worship. This is manifested in their character and behaviour with the creation of Allah, and how they deal with the trials and tribulations of life.

The Prophet (peace be upon him) said, "Shall I not tell you about the best of you?" They said, "Of course." The Prophet said, "Those who, if they are seen, they remind you of Allah. (Albani)

Dawah is our duty

As Muslims, our belief in Allah and love for His creation demands that we try and save people from themselves, by telling them about the most precious thing we have, our faith. Our duty is to spread the message of Islam to others (Dawah),

to help them find salvation, as was the duty of the Prophets, and after them, their communities.

The Prophet (peace be upon him) said, "Verily, the parable of myself and the people is that of a man who kindled a fire. When it lighted what was around it, moths and insects started falling into the fire. The man tried to pull them out, but they overcame him and rushed into it. I take hold of your belts to keep you from falling in, yet you rush into it." (Bukhari)

There should always be a group among you that calls people to what is best, enjoins the common good and forbids evil; this group of people are the successful. (Qur'an 3:104)

Whose speech can be better than the one who calls to Allah and acts righteously and states openly: "I am a Muslim." (Qur'an 41:33)

But while doing this we must remember two things:

- All we can do is spread the message, it is not up to us whether someone believes in Allah and accepts Islam or not, that is up to Allah alone.

- *Messenger, you can't guide who you love. But Allah guides anyone He chooses. And Allah knows the guided. (Qur'an 28:56)*

- We must not look down on or persecute people for their lack of faith or belief in atheism.

- *Invite to your Lord's way wisely; teaching in a pleasant manner, and debating with courtesy... (Qur'an 16:125)*

Allah is not affected by our belief or disbelief in Him

Finally, we must remember that whether we, anyone else, or in fact the entire creation, was to believe in Allah or not, it makes no difference to whether Allah exists or not. His existence is not dependent or affected in any way by our belief or disbelief in Him.

The Prophet (peace be upon him) said: "Allah the Exalted and Glorious, said: '...O My slaves, you can neither do Me any harm nor can you do Me any good. O My slaves, were the first of you and the last of you, the human of you and Jinn of you to be as pious as the most pious heart of any man of you, that would not increase My domain a thing. O My slaves, were the first of you, and the last of you, the human of you and the Jinn of you to be as wicked as the most wicked heart of any man of you, that would not decrease My domain in a thing. O My slaves, were the first of you and the last of you, the human of you and the Jinn of you to stand in one place and make a request of Me, and were I to give everyone what he requested, that would not decrease what I have...'" (Muslim)

This is the ultimate aim of Shaitan, to make as many people as he can disbelieve in Allah, since death while in that state will cause them to enter Hell, which is his final destination. How ironic, given that he himself knows with absolute certainty that Allah exists.

Another comparison of the hypocrites is Satan; he says to man, "Don't believe," and when he disbelieves, Satan says to him, "I disown you, I fear Allah, the Lord of the worlds." The punishment for both is the Fire where they will live forever, the reward for the wrongdoers. (Qur'an 59:16-17)

Conclusion

As we have discussed, belief in God is not irrational and indeed, can be considered a part of human nature. As theists we are often challenged to prove the existence of God but this is not something that is meant to be proved, like a scientific fact. If this were possible there would be no need for 'faith'. After all, if God wanted to provide irrefutable proof of His existence to everyone, He could very easily do so. Instead, it is a personal matter, for individual reflection, for each and every one of us to decide for ourselves. By doing so, this is what gives our faith value, and gives us the conviction to not only live our own lives with the primary purpose of pleasing our Creator, but to encourage others to also ponder this question, to find faith and achieve salvation.

Questions

- What does having faith mean?

- Can we prove that Allah exists?

- Does the God of the gaps argument apply to Muslim belief in Allah; if not, why not?

- Do you have a personal relationship with Allah? What is your level of certainty that He exists?

- If something terrible was to happen in your life, would it affect your faith in Allah?

Activities

- Do some research regarding the miracles Allah granted to different Prophets (peace be upon them all), imagine how it would have been to witness them

- Listen to online lectures, read books, or study with a teacher the Tafsir of the Qur'an to appreciate its miraculous nature

- Find out what Dawah projects (to provide people with knowledge of Islam) are being carried out in your area and think about how you can get involved

1 . 2

One God, Different Religions

Objectives

- To understand that the religion of Islam did not begin with the Prophet Muhammad (peace be upon him)

- To explore how other major world religions may have had an Islamic origin

- To consider how you could have an interfaith dialogue to learn about other faiths and teach others about Islam

Keywords

- Religion

- Prophet

- Revelation

- Interfaith

Why did Allah create the Universe?

Allah says He was a hidden treasure and wanted to be discovered, and so He created the Universe and then mankind. But like any treasure, Allah remains hidden. He is not out in the open, we cannot see Him, we cannot hear Him, we cannot talk to Him or touch Him in the same way we can with anything that is part of His creation. Allah made the life of this world a test for us, if we please Him, He will reward us with eternity in Paradise. If we displease Him, He will punish us with eternity in Hell. But how do we know what pleases or displeases our Creator? How do we pass this test? How can we listen to, talk to, and experience Allah?

Islam – the religion of all Prophets

Allah has a system of doing things. This system involves sending Prophets to communities, sometimes with a Revelation in order to give them this information. In one Hadith, the number 124,000 is given for the number of Prophets from the Prophet Adam to our Prophet Muhammad (peace be upon them all), but regardless of the exact count, all the Prophets taught the religion of Islam (which can be translated as peace through submission to Allah). However as human society developed, the teachings of each Prophet and the Revelations they were sent with all slightly differed while having the same central message i.e. to follow the Prophet, only worship the one true God, Allah in the way that He instructed us to, to do good deeds and refrain from committing sins, to develop good character and help the creation of Allah. For this reason, we believe they were all Muslims, preaching the version of Islam Allah gave to them.

Corruption of Prophetic teachings and Divine Revelations

In the Qur'an, Allah tells us the stories of some of the Prophets and how only a few people from their communities believed in the message they were sent with. After the Prophets passed away, over time as generations passed, the Revelation that they came with and their teachings were changed as those in power wanted to maintain their comfortable lives and didn't like having to follow uncomfortable rules.

"Do you expect them to believe you when a group of them hears the words of Allah and, after understanding them, deliberately changes them?" (Qur'an 2:75)

"Some of them twist their tongues when reciting from the Book to make you think it is from the Book, even though it forms no part of the Book, and they say, "This is from Allah," even though it is not from Allah, and they knowingly tell lies against Allah." (Qur'an 3:78)

The Prophet Musa (peace be upon him) came to the Jews with the Taurat (Torah). After he passed away, Allah tells us how over time, some Jewish leaders stopped following his teachings and changed the Taurat.

When Allah sent the Prophet Isa (peace be upon him), he was sent to the Jews with a new revelation, the Injil (Gospel). But most of the Jews did not believe in him as a Prophet, the ones who did however, became Christians. He was eventually taken up by Allah into the Heavens and again, over time some Christian leaders changed the Injil. They taught that the Prophet Isa (peace be upon him) had been killed (crucified on the cross), resurrected back to life three days later, and that he was actually God, or the son of God. Similarly, when the Prophet Muhammad (peace be upon him) was sent by Allah as the final Prophet with the Qur'an, most of the Jews and Christians refused to believe in him as a Prophet, even though the original Taurat and Injil had contained descriptions of the final Prophet and how to recognise him.

Those who follow the Messenger, the untutored Prophet who is mentioned in the Torah and Gospel... (Qur'an 7:157)

Jews, Christians and Muslims

This explains why we have Judaism, Christianity and Islam, even though as Muslims we believe the Prophet Musa and the Prophet Isa (peace be upon them both) were both Muslims, preaching the version of Islam Allah sent them with. When the Injil was revealed to the Prophet Isa all the Jews should have followed him and become Christians. Similarly, when the Qur'an was revealed to the Prophet Muhammad all the Christians should have followed him and become Muslims.

Since the religion, the version of Islam Allah sent His Prophets with, changed over time, and the previous Prophetic teachings and Revelations were modified, some major differences emerged between the three Abrahamic faiths. Having said this, Muslims still believe the Word of Allah is contained within the Taurat and Injil, but will only follow it if it is also verified within the Qur'an or a Hadith of the Prophet Muhammad (peace be upon him). This is why we do not live our life according to the commandments of previous Revelations.

The Qur'an however has not been changed since Allah has taken it upon Himself to prevent this from happening. He states in the Qur'an itself:

We revealed the Reminder, and We are its Protectors. (Qur'an 15:9)

As proof of this, the copies of the Mus'haf we have today and the oldest versions discovered from close to the time the Prophet was alive (nearly 1400 years ago), are identical.

Other major World religions

This explains why we have the three Abrahamic faiths but what about other major world religions like Hinduism, Buddhism, and Sikhism? Hinduism and Buddhism are ancient religions, thousands of years old. If we look at their teachings, many of them are similar to those found in the Abrahamic faiths so it is probable that these religions started as an ancient version of Islam, by a Prophet or Prophets sent with Revelation that we have not been told about in the Qur'an:

There were messengers that We told you about, and there are other messengers that We haven't told you about... (Qur'an 4:164)

Supporting this theory, we can find descriptions matching the Prophet Muhammad (peace be upon him) and his companions (may Allah be pleased with them all) in the Hindu holy books. Many Buddhist teachings are also similar to those found in Tassawuf, the inward dimension of Islam which teaches us how to purify our soul and draw closer to Allah, which all Prophets taught their disciples. Buddhists don't believe in a God but do believe in an Ultimate Reality, which we can reach through meditation and a life of asceticism (giving up our desires for this temporary world).

Like with Judaism and Christianity, over time there would have been changes made to these religions, and the majority of followers would not have followed subsequent Prophets that Allah sent with new Revelations, and so we still have these ancient religions but no longer upon the right path (Siratul Mustaqim).

Sikhism is a newer religion, started about 500 years ago by Guru Nanak, who was followed by nine other Gurus, and their holy book is called the Guru Granth Sahib. Since Guru Nanak was born after the Prophet Muhammad (peace be upon him), it is impossible for him to be a Prophet, as stated within the Qur'an:

Muhammad is not father of anyone of your men, he is the Messenger of Allah and the Seal of the Prophets, a final Prophet. (Qur'an 33:40)

This also means the Guru Granth Sahib cannot be Revelation from Allah. However, if we look at the teachings of Sikhism they are similar to what Islam teaches us. In fact, many of the Gurus including Guru Nanak had very close Muslim friends who were of the Awliyah Allah (friends of Allah, or saints). One of these Awliyah Allah was Syedina Baba Farid (may Allah have mercy upon him), and some of his writings have been included in the Guru Granth Sahib.

However, as Muslims we believe that a revelation from Allah cannot be changed except by Allah Himself, which He does by sending another Prophet. The Prophet Muhammad (peace be upon him) was the final Prophet sent with the final Revelation, the Qur'an:

...Today, I have completed your religion for you; I gave My favour in full, and I am happy that Submission to My will is your religion... (Qur'an 5:3)

Allah is telling us He has perfected our religion for us, thereby instructing mankind to follow it until the Day of Judgement. Therefore, no further changes are required necessitating future Prophets or Revelations. So Muslims would agree with the parts of Sikhism which match with the teachings of Islam, but disagree with the rest.

Interfaith dialogue

As Muslims, talking with people of other faiths to learn more about their beliefs and practices, and educating them about Islam is a praiseworthy act. But we should try not to argue about how their religion is wrong and ours is right. This will drive most people further away from Islam, not towards it.

Invite to your Lord's way wisely; teaching in a pleasant manner, and debating with courtesy... (Qur'an 16:125)

If we have arguments like this it is very easy to say the wrong thing. We might insult their Prophet (peace be upon them all) or holy figure, which can cause them to insult our Prophet (peace be upon him) or Allah:

Believers, don't insult anything they worship beside Allah, they will insult Allah out of hostility and ignorance. (Qur'an 6:108)

They might say we believe something and without being sure if what they have said is true, we might deny it or try to explain it in a way that is incorrect, thereby damaging our faith. If we are asked a question about our religion that we do not know the answer to or are unsure about, we should have no hesitation in saying that we do not know, that we will find out the answer and get back to them. We should then ask an Islamic scholar, which will help increase our own knowledge, and that of the person who asked us the question.

A word of warning

We should also never judge someone and say that they are going to Hell because they are not a Muslim. This is not our job, only Allah knows if someone is going to Heaven or Hell. Some of the biggest enemies of the Prophet (peace be upon him) ended up converting to Islam and becoming his Sahabahcompanions (e.g. Syedina Abu Sufyaan, may Allah be pleased with him). There are people who have spent their whole lives as followers of another religion, or atheists, who convert to

Islam in their old age, and by doing so all their bad deeds are forgiven and they die with less sins than people who lived their whole life as Muslims. In fact, the Prophet (peace be upon him) told us that we have no guarantee that even if we live our whole life as Muslims, that we will die as a Muslim, and so this should be something we pray for every day.

Conclusion

As Muslims we believe in the final Prophet of Allah, Muhammad (peace be upon him) and the final Revelation, the Qur'an, which Allah has promised to protect from being changed or corrupted. There are many other religions in the world, many of which are older versions of Islam given to previous Prophets, whose teachings and Revelations have been changed over time. If we want to teach people about Islam the best way to do it is by learning about it ourselves and living our life in the beautiful way of our Prophet (peace be upon him). When people see our good character and realise this is what Islam teaches, they will want to find out more about it and if Allah blesses them, may even become Muslims themselves. If instead we argue and fight with people because they are not Muslims, if we look down on or persecute them, then because of us they will hate Muslims and we will be driving them away from Islam.

Questions

- Why did Allah send Prophets (peace be upon them all)?

- What are the names of the Revelations we are told about in the Qur'an?

- Can we follow commandments contained within the holy books of other religions?

- Why are there similarities and differences between Judaism, Christianity and Islam?

- How should we treat someone who is of a different faith?

- What is the best way to do Dawah (spreading the message of Islam)?

Activities

- Talk to a friend who is of a different faith to learn about their religion and how it affects their everyday life

- Talk to a friend about Islam, and how it affects your everyday life

- Find out if there are interfaith groups in your area that you could join

- Go to a place of worship of a different faith and think about how it is similar to and different from a Mosque

- Invite a friend to come to the Mosque to show them how Muslims pray and what other activities take place in the Mosque

- Treat people with good manners, and if someone praises you, thank them and tell them you are trying to copy the behaviour of the Prophet (peace be upon him) and act on the teachings of the Qur'an

1 . 3
The Qur'an and Hadith

Prepare for this topic

Objectives

- To understand the objections raised against the genuineness of the Qur'an and Hadith

- To explore the history of how we came to have the Mus'haf

- To consider the scholarship involved in the sciences of Hadith verification

Keywords

- Qur'an

- Mus'haf

- Hadith

- Sanad

Common objections raised against the genuineness of the Qur'an

Some non-Muslims assert that the Qur'an we have today may be different from what was revealed to the Prophet (peace be upon him) because it was not written down during his lifetime. Also, since he spoke it to his companions (may Allah be pleased with them all), and it was transmitted to others via speech, it would have changed in the way a message gets changed during a game of Chinese whispers. They argue that the reason we don't see different versions of the Qur'an today (as with the Bible) is because many years after the Prophet was alive (peace be upon him), all the different versions were burnt so only one version would be copied and passed down from one generation to the next. But there is no proof that this version is identical to what was revealed to the Prophet Muhammad (peace be upon him), and the fact that there were different versions which had to be gotten rid of, proves this.

The Qur'an was written down during the life of the Prophet (peace be upon him)

The Qur'an was revealed to the Prophet Muhammad (peace be upon him), over a period of 23 years. When verses of the Qur'an were revealed, he recited them to his companions (may Allah be pleased with them all) and instructed them where the verses fit in relation to others. Many companions (may Allah be pleased with them all) had memorised either parts, or all of the Qur'an during the Prophet's lifetime. The literate ones would also write it down on cleaned pieces of bone, leather, or leaves, which were carefully stored. Therefore, although the oral tradition was the main method of memorisation and transmission, the written tradition was also used as it was being revealed, during the lifetime of the Prophet (peace be upon him).

The strength of the oral tradition

Although the main method of transmission of the Qur'an from one person to another was oral, it is incorrect to compare this to a game of Chinese whispers where a message is whispered along a chain of people with the aim of ending up with a different message by the end of it. Whenever a Qur'anic verse was revealed, the Prophet (peace be upon him) would recite it to the companions that were with him, several of them would learn it and then check with the Prophet (peace be upon him) that they had learnt it correctly. Afterwards, other companions who were not present during the Revelation, would come to the Prophet (peace be upon him) or the companions who had memorised the verses, and hear it and learn it from them. Previously revealed verses of the Qur'an were also constantly being recited by the Prophet (peace be upon him), in the daily congregational prayers, and to teach the companions.

So the entirety of the Qur'an that was revealed up to any point in time was being recited by the Prophet and his companions to each other, and if there were any mistakes in what a companion was reciting it would be corrected, and if there were any differences of opinion between companions these would be taken to the Prophet (peace be upon

him) for resolution. The Prophet's memorisation of the Qur'an was guaranteed by Allah Himself, and each year during Ramadan, he would recite it with the Archangel Jibra'il (may Allah be pleased with him).

Messenger, don't read the Qur'an too fast to memorise it. We are responsible for its compilation and recital. So when We recite it, then follow its recitation. It is also Our responsibility to explain it clearly to you. (Qur'an 75:16-18)

We will teach you the Qur'an so you will not forget it... (Qur'an 87:6)

Syedina Ibn Abbas (may Allah be pleased with him) said, "The (Angel) Jibra'il used to meet the Prophet (peace be upon him) every night in Ramadan and study the Qur'an with him." (Bukhari)

So the oral tradition was not a one-way transmission along a line of people, but a constant back and forth transmission between an interconnected web of people. The Arabs of the time were also renowned for their excellent memories, able to recite hundreds or even thousands of lines of poetry by heart.

This method of transmission continues up to today, even though the written Qur'an (the Mus'haf) is commonplace. All around the world there are countless Muslims who

have memorised the Qur'an (Huffaz), of all different ages, races, cultures, countries, and languages. Yet every word of the Qur'an they recite is identical. If one of them was to make a mistake during their recitation, for example during the congregational prayer, there are Huffaz standing behind them to correct them.

Collation of the Qur'an into the Mus'haf

During the reign of Syedina Abu-Bakr (may Allah be pleased with him) many Huffaz were martyred during the battle of Yamama (may Allah be pleased with them all), and so the Mus'haf was collected and compiled. By the time of Syedina Usman's caliphate (may Allah be pleased with him), Islam had spread through many Arab lands, where the dialect and pronunciation varied. This led to accusations that the Qur'an was being changed. So the Caliph formed a committee to create duplicates of the original Mus'haf in the Quraishi dialect, which would get rid of the problem of different pronunciations. This was recited in front of the Muslims of Medina, since this was the place where most companions who had heard the Qur'an recited by the Prophet himself still lived, before copies were sent to the rest of the Islamic world. Any copies of the Mus'haf which were not identical to this one were burnt (a respectful way of disposing of copies of the Qur'an).

Unlike the previous Revelations which were changed, however, Allah has taken it upon Himself to safeguard the Qur'an:

"We revealed the Reminder, and We are its Protectors." (Qur'an 15:9)

The Qur'an we have today, more

than 1400 years after the time of the Prophet (peace be upon him), is identical to the very oldest copies of the Mus'haf that have been found, from the time of the first and second-generation Muslims (may Allah be pleased with them all).

What about Hadith of the Prophet (peace be upon him)?

Some Muslims believe that the Qur'an has remained unchanged since the time of the Prophet (peace be upon him) as Allah has protected it, and that anything other than the Qur'an, such as the Sunnah and Hadith of the Prophet (peace be upon him) is unreliable and in fact, unnecessary.

Allah sent Revelation to guide humanity. But to gain this guidance, we have different methods to help understand the Qur'an. For example, some verses are either:

- straightforward and don't need any further explanation (although even they have many deeper meanings which are not obvious to the common person)

- not so simple but we can find an explanation for them in other parts of the Qur'an or

- explained by the Prophet (peace be upon him) to his companions (peace be upon him), through his teachings (Hadith) and how he lived his life (Sunnah).

When the wife of the Prophet (peace be upon him), Syedatuna Aisha (may Allah be pleased with her) was asked to describe his character, she said his character was the Qur'an:

Syedina Qatadah reported: I said to Syedatuna Aisha (may Allah be pleased with them both), "O mother of the believers, tell me about the character of the Messenger of Allah, peace and blessings be upon him." Syedatuna Aisha said, "Have you not read the Quran?" I said, "Of course." Syedatuna Aisha said, "Verily, the character of the Prophet of Allah was the Quran." (Muslim)

In other words, he lived his life doing everything exactly as Allah has told us to in the Qur'an.

Understanding the Qur'an through Hadith of the Prophet (peace be upon him)

This is one of the wisdoms of Allah in sending a Revelation with a Prophet rather than by itself. The life of the Prophet and his teachings help to interpret the Revelation for the community at the time and for generations afterwards. For example, in the Qur'an it tells us to perform Salah (five daily prayers), Zakat (yearly charity), Sawm (fasting) and Hajj (pilgrimage to Makkah). But it is only within the Hadith of the Prophet (peace be upon him) that we find instructions on how to perform these Fard (obligatory) acts. Otherwise we would not know how many prayers to perform each day, what actions we needed to do and what we needed to recite during each action, and how many Rak'at (units of prayer) each prayer contains. We would not know how much of our wealth we needed to give in charity each year, who qualifies to receive the money, and how we work out what is our savings and what isn't. We would not know what things are and aren't allowed while we are fasting, nor about all the different rites we need to complete during Hajj or Umrah.

Allah tells us to follow the Prophet (peace be upon him)

In the Qur'an, Allah tells the Prophet (peace be upon him) that he has the most excellent character, as an instruction for us to try to emulate it. Allah also tells us that the Prophet (peace be upon him) speaks only the truth which comes from Allah:

By the shining star when it came down, your companion is neither misguided nor deluded. He doesn't speak from his desire. This is a Revelation sent down... (Qur'an 53:1-4)

Some Muslims think this verse is only referring to the Prophet (peace be upon him) in relation to Qur'anic verses. But obviously, it must also apply to:

- any explanations he gave to his companions (may Allah be pleased with them all) regarding the Revelation

- Hadith Kudsi (where Allah's speech was relayed directly by the Prophet, but did not form part of the Qur'an) and

- nearly everything the Prophet (peace be upon him) said and did since the companions used to follow whatever he told them, and would try to copy every single thing he did, as a way to live their life in a way that would please Allah.

If Allah was not guiding his speech and actions, the Prophet himself would have stopped his companions from copying him or acting upon what he said.

Messenger, don't read the Qur'an too fast to memorise it. We are responsible for its compilation and recital. So when We recite it, then follow its recitation. It is also Our responsibility to explain it clearly to you. (Qur'an 75:16-18)

This explains why Allah included the following instructions within the Qur'an:

...If you disagree over something, then refer it to Allah and the Messenger, that is if you believe in Allah and the Last Day: that's the best solution. (Qur'an 4:59)

Whoever obeys the Messenger has obeyed Allah... (Qur'an 4:80)

...Whatever the Messenger gives you, take it. And whatever he forbids you from, leave it... (Qur'an 59:7)

Scholars of the Qur'an tell us that these verses were not just revealed for the companions (may Allah be pleased with them all), but all Muslims until the Day of Judgement. Therefore, Allah is telling us quite clearly, in His Qur'an, the importance of following the Sunnah and Hadith of the Prophet (peace be upon him).

The risk of Hadith forgeries

This importance however became open to abuse after his death as forgeries began to appear. If someone could support what they were doing by saying the Prophet (peace be upon him) had allowed it, this was a way to gain authority and convince others. This could easily have led to the religion splitting into many groups, each using fake Hadith to support the society they wanted to create. So Muslim scholars had to come up with a system to determine whether or not a Hadith was authentic i.e. how likely it was that it was said by the Prophet (peace be upon).

The Prophet knew that there was a danger of this happening, and so warned us that it would earn Allah's anger:

The Prophet (peace be upon him) said: "Telling lies about me is not like telling lies about anyone else. Whoever tells lies about me deliberately, let him take his place in Hell." (Bukhari)

Repeatedly in the Qur'an Allah tells us not to just believe anything we hear and repeat it to others, but to check whether it is true, to ask for proof, to find witnesses, and if we are not sure, to leave it, because otherwise we will be led astray and will lead others astray.

Believers, if some crooked person brings you news, then check it in case you cause harm to others ignorantly, and then later regret what you did. (Qur'an 49:6)

The science of verifying Hadith

This is a multistep process:

The first step is to check that the Hadith has a Sanad – this is the chain of narrators going back to the Prophet (peace be upon him). Normally it takes the form of 'person

X narrated from person Y who was told by his father Z, that the Prophet (peace be upon him) said...'.

If the Hadith has a Sanad, the next step is for the scholar to investigate whether it was possible for the Hadith to have been transmitted along this chain. To do this they use biographical books written about people who were known to transmit Hadith. They would check to see if the people within the Sanad were mentioned in these books. When were they alive, where did they live, and did they travel? This is to check whether their lives had overlapped and it was possible that they could have met in order to transmit the Hadith. The scholar would also examine other Hadith transmitted by the same people within the Sanad, to see if they too had been classified as authentic.

The third step is to consider how trustworthy each person in the Sanad is. Obviously if someone is known to have been a liar, their inclusion in a Sanad would raise doubts over the authenticity of the Hadith. But there are other ways to check this as well. For example, are the Hadith a certain person transmits always different from the same one transmitted by a trustworthy person? If there is only one person transmitting a certain Hadith from their teacher when that teacher is known to have other students who also transmit – this raises the question as to why none of the other students transmitted it as well? As well as truthfulness, the ability to memorise accurately, and the moral character of the person is also examined.

Finally, the scholar will also consider how many different Sanad a Hadith has. The more people a Hadith is transmitted through at each level of its transmission, in other words, the more sources a Hadith has, the more likely it is to be authentic.

Another aspect of verifying a Hadith which is independent of its Sanad, is to check its text (Matn) or meaning, to see if it is in agreement with the Qur'an and other authenticated Hadith. However, even if it seems to be saying something contradictory, before disregarding it as a fabricated Hadith it should be checked whether it relates to a specific time, place or person, in which case the Prophet (peace be upon him) might have been making an exception to a rule. The Hadith should also not contradict historical or scientific facts, or common sense and logic (keeping in mind that science, common sense and logic are not absolutes, but dependent on the time we live in, and can change significantly over centuries.

Hadith classification

Using this system, Hadith have been given different classifications:

Sahih (authentic) means the Hadith has a Sanad in which each person was totally trustworthy, had an excellent memory, and lived at a common time and place so they could have met.

Hasan (good) means the Hadith is similar in authenticity to a Sahih Hadith, but there is something about it which means it is labelled as Hasan rather than Sahih. For example, the memory of one of the narrators in the Sanad was good rather than excellent. But if a Hasan Hadith has several Sanad, it moves up to the category of Sahih. Both Sahih and Hasan Hadith are used for religious rulings alongside the Qur'an.

Da'if (weak) means the Hadith does not fulfil the criteria to be labelled Sahih or Hasan. Reasons for this include a break in the Sanad, criticisms of one of the narrators (such as not having a good memory), and/or the Hadith seems to be saying something different from another Hadith which is Sahih or Hasan. But this does not mean the Hadith is a forgery. Within all the Da'if Hadith, it is only those labelled Mawdu that are determined to be forgeries (in other words, not said by the Prophet - peace be upon him). This means that even though Da'if Hadith cannot be used for religious

rulings, stories in them can be used to learn lessons and teach others, and if they mention Nawafil acts of worship (extra, non-obligatory acts), we can perform these as a source of blessing.

Mutawatir means a Hadith has many Sanad at each level of transmission. Therefore, it must be authentic since it is impossible that all the transmitters made a conspiracy to tell the same lie without being discovered.

Aziz means the Hadith has two Sanad at each level of transmission.

Gharib means the Hadith has just one Sanad.

Great Hadith scholars and Hadith collections

Therefore, the study of Hadith goes hand in hand with their verification, and this is a science which scholars spend their whole lives studying (Ulum al-Hadith – sciences of Hadith, and Ilm al-Rijal - biographical studies). Some of the greatest scholars in this field are famous due to having created collections of Hadith in books which have been relied upon over centuries by the Muslim Ummah.

For example, Imam Bukhari (may Allah have mercy upon him), who lived roughly 200 years after the time of the Prophet (peace be upon him) travelled from a young age, meeting scholars and learning Hadith and their Sanad. He knew more than 600,000 Hadith which he studied for over 16 years, using strict criteria to decide upon the roughly 7,000 Hadith he eventually put into his book, Sahih al-Bukhari.

One of Imam Bukhari's students was Imam Muslim (may Allah have mercy upon them both). He also travelled widely, collecting Hadith from many scholars and evaluating them. He is said to have known over 300,000 Hadith, from which he chose roughly 4,000 to put into his book, Sahih Muslim.

The aim of both of these scholars was to create collections of Sahih Hadith over which there was no doubt regarding their authenticity. But this is not to say they included all Sahih

Hadith within their collections, and they themselves never claimed this (in other words, you cannot say that if a Hadith is not included within Sahih al-Bukhari or Sahih Muslim, that it is not Sahih).

Four other famous scholars and their Hadith collections include:

Imam Abu Dawood (may Allah be pleased with him) who wrote Sunan Abu Dawood containing over 5,000 Hadith out of the over 500,000 that he collected over 20 years.

Jami at-Tirmidhi written by Imam at-Tirmidhi, another student of Imam Bukhari (may Allah be pleased with them both) containing nearly 4,000 Hadith. He also wrote the Shama'il Muhammadiyah (commonly known as Shama'il Tirmidhi) in which he collected specific Hadith about how the Prophet (peace be upon him) looked and his character.

Sunan an-Nisai (also known as Sunan al-Sughra) written by Imam an-Nisai containing over 5,000 Hadith

Sunan ibn Majah written by Imam ibn Majah containing over 4,000 Hadith.

I have mentioned these six books (Kutub al-Sittah) because for Sunni Muslims these six are the most authentic collections of Hadith, and their authors are some of the most expert Hadith scholars within the Muslim Ummah. Other great scholars have spent their lives studying these books, writing commentaries about them and the ways in which particular Hadith were selected (e.g. Fath al-Bari; the most comprehensive commentary on Sahih Bukhari, by Ibn Hajar al-Asqalani, may Allah have mercy upon him). These six books however are not the only ones. There are many more collections of Hadith that also contain authentic Hadith.

Conclusion

Allah promised to keep the Qur'an from being corrupted or changed, and He did this not only through the hard work of scholars who spent their whole lives learning the Qur'an and its meaning and teaching it to others, but also through the scholars who spent their lives learning, classifying and collecting the Hadith of the Prophet (peace be upon him). This is because religion needs both Prophet and Revelation, as is the system of Allah, and so both of these things need to be preserved until the Day of Judgement.

Questions

- How was the Qur'an transmitted during the Prophet's lifetime and after he passed away?

- Was the decision to compile it made during his lifetime?

- Why were copies of the Mus'haf burnt during the Caliphate of Syedina Usman (may Allah be pleased with him)?

- How old are the oldest copies of the Mus'haf that have been found, and have any differences been found between them and copies of the Mus'haf that are being printed today?

- Do Muslims need anything else to help them understand the Qur'an?

- Why was the science of hadith important for the early Muslims?

- What are the different aspects of a Hadith that a scholar will check to determine its authenticity?

- If a Hadith is Da'if (weak), i.e. not Sahih or Hasan, does that mean it is a forgery?

- What can and cannot a Da'if Hadith be used for?

Activities

- Gather everyone in your family. Explain that you have something important to tell them which they will need to remember. Give them a short sentence, and ask them to repeat it to each other as well. The next day, ask them about it and if they make a mistake in remembering, remind them. On another day, play a game of Chinese whispers with your friends using the same short sentence. Consider how different these two ways are of passing on information to other people.

- Find a museum which houses an old copy of the Mus'haf and learn about its history.

- Read Taraweeh prayer in a Mosque during Ramadan. Note how, whenever the Imam makes a mistake in his recitation, someone is there to correct him.

- Look at the way Hadith scholars have arranged their books in chapters, and chosen Hadith for each chapter based on their subject

- Read about Hadith which seem to contradict each other or the Qur'an, and how scholars have resolved these differences

- Read about how and why a specific Hadith has been determined to be Sahih, Hasan or Da'if

1 . 4

Different Sects and Schools of Religious Law

Objectives

- To understand the difference between a religious sect and school of religious law

- To explore the similarities and differences between different Islamic sects

- To consider the extent of learning required to become a Mujtahid

Keywords

- Sect

- Sunni

- Shia

- Madhab

What are religious sects?

Different religions can be thought of as maps, given to us by Allah to guide us to our destination, which is the pleasure of Allah and His Paradise. If we look at other religions, a recurring pattern is that their followers are split into groups. When groups of followers understand the map of their religion differently from each other they are called 'sects'.

The role of the Prophets (peace be upon them all)

Whenever Allah sent a new Prophet (peace be upon them all), their people would have lots of questions for them. They wanted to find out how the new message they were sent with was different to the old religions that were being practiced at the time. The people who came to the new Prophet truly wanting to understand their message and worship Allah would be blessed by Allah to become believers and companions of the Prophet. Once they had accepted the Prophet as the Messenger of Allah, any disagreements or problems in understanding the religion would be brought to the Prophet, who, guided by Allah, would tell people what to do and what to believe. Therefore, during the life of the Prophet, different sects could not occur, because the Prophet ensured the true believers had a unified, true understanding of the map of religion they were sent with.

Religious disagreements

However, after a Prophet passed away, sorting out disagreements was not as simple. It is easier if the

disagreement is about something fundamental to the religion, like a commandment within the Revelation, or something the Prophet told his companions quite clearly.

For example, after the Prophet Muhammad (peace be upon him) passed away and Syedina Abu-Bakr (may Allah be pleased with him) became the leader of the Muslims, some Arab tribes refused to pay Zakat, arguing that this was only meant to be paid to the Prophet. Syedina Abu-Bakr warned them that if they did not pay he would go to war with them, because he would not allow them to change the religion of the Prophet (peace be upon him).

Furthermore, some people started calling themselves Prophets, that they had been sent by Allah after the Prophet Muhammad (peace be upon him) and everyone should now follow them. Under Abu-Bakr's leadership, the Muslims waged war against these false prophets and their followers believing they would have split the religion apart. These things did not result in sects within Islam because they were clearly against the Qur'an and teachings of the Prophet (peace be upon him).

The Ahmadiyya movement

In modern times a man called Mirza Ghulam Ahmad claimed to be a Prophet of Allah. He said that the Prophet Muhammad (peace be upon him) was the final Messenger but not the final Prophet. A Messenger is the name given to a Prophet who was sent with a new message or new set of rules (in the form of Revelation) from Allah. For example, Syedina Musa was a Messenger, while his brother, Syedina Haroon was a Prophet.

Mirza Ghulam Ahmad said he was such a Prophet, and that such Prophets would keep being sent until the Day of Judgement. The people who follow him are known as the Ahmadiyya movement, also known as Qaidiani. They believe that Allah described the Prophet Muhammad as being the 'seal of the Prophets' in the Qur'an because he has the highest rank and is the most beloved to Allah. According to them, this means that Allah will not send any more Messengers because there cannot be another or a better message than Islam, however, this

does not mean that Allah will not send any more Prophets to reinforce the message of Islam and ensure Muslims are following their religion correctly.

Ahmadis are considered non-Muslims because they disagree with a fundamental belief of Islam, that the Prophet Muhammad (peace be upon him) was the last Prophet of Allah, and after him no new Prophets would be sent (with or without new laws), about which Islamic scholars from all sects are in agreement:

Muhammad is not the father of any man among you; rather, he is the Messenger of God and the Seal of the prophets... (Qur'an 33:40)

The Prophet (peace be upon him) said, "The chain of Messengers and Prophets has come to an end. There shall be no Messenger nor Prophet after me." (Tirmidhi)

The Sunni and Shia sects

The two biggest sects within Islam are Sunni and Shia, which themselves have many smaller sub-sects. The major point of difference between Sunni and Shia is who should have become the first caliph after the death of the Prophet (peace be upon him).

Shia believe:

■ The caliph should have been Syedina Ali, the cousin of the Prophet (peace be upon him) and the husband of his daughter Syedatuna Fatima (may Allah be pleased with them both).

■ Syedina Ali was the greatest companion of the Prophet (peace be upon him).

■ There are certain Hadith of the Prophet which show the

incredible levels of faith and knowledge Syedina Ali was blessed with and so the Prophet wanted him to lead the Muslims after his death.

Sunnis believe:

■ The agreed opinion of the companions (may Allah be pleased with them all) after the death of the Prophet (peace be upon him), was that Syedina Abu-Bakr should lead the Muslims, and this is what happened according to the will of Allah.

■ The Prophet (peace be upon him) told us about the amazing qualities of many of his closest companions, which tells us how Allah had blessed them all in their own ways

■ Alongside Syedina Ali, the four closest companions of the Prophet (peace be upon him) included Syedina Abu-Bakr, Umar and Usman (may Allah be pleased with them all). They were all also close family members of the Prophet, Syedina Abu-Bakr and Umar's daughters were married to the Prophet (and so were his fathers-in-law), and Syedina Usman had married two of the Prophet's daughters (and so was his son in law alongside Syedina Ali).

In recent times (the last 300 years or so), the division between Sunni and Shia has grown, leading to hatred and fighting and many now even believe the other sect is outside the fold of Islam and can't call themselves Muslims. A very large number of the Shia population believe that some of the Prophet's companions and a few of his wives (may Allah be pleased with them all) betrayed Syedina Ali after the Prophet's death. However, it is a historical fact that Syedina Ali gave his allegiance to Syedina Abu-Bakr six months after the Prophet passed away and was perhaps the most trusted advisor of the first three caliphs (Syedina Abu-Bakr, Syedina Umar, and Syedina Usman). In fact, Sunnis consider it a huge blessing for the caliphs that they had such an amazing advisor as Syedina Ali to help them during the difficult times after the Prophet (peace be upon him) passed away and Islam was spreading so rapidly, bringing new challenges. Another historical fact is that Syedina Ali named some of his sons after the first three caliphs, Abu-Bakr, Umar and Usman.

Other differences:

■ **The Ahl al-bayt or the family of the Prophet.**

Both Sunni and Shia agree that this includes Syedina Ali, Fatima, Hassan and Hussain (may Allah be pleased with them all) and their descendants. However, while Shia believe that the Ahl al-Bayt only contain these members of his family, Sunnis believe it also includes his wives (as mentioned in the Qur'an), and other children.

Wives of the Prophet, you are not like other women...Allah wants to remove all blight from you as you are the Prophet's household, and to keep you pure... (Qur'an 33:32-33)

■ **Following Hadith.**

Shia mainly follow Hadith and Sunnah of the Prophet (peace be upon him) which have been transmitted through the Ahl al-bayt. They only refer to Hadith transmitted by the wives or companions of the Prophet (may Allah be pleased with them all) when there is a need to.

■ **The Imam System**

Shias call Syedina Ali, Hassan, Hussain and nine descendants of Syedina Hussain 'Imams' because they believe:

• they have superiority over all other Muslims in faith and knowledge

• the spiritual and worldly leaders of the Muslims have always been these 12 Imams.

• each Imam was chosen by the previous Imam, and the new Imam does not commit sins due to the faith and knowledge they have been blessed with.

• the last Imam is Imam Mahdi, who has already been born but has been hidden from the world (like Syedina Khizr) and will come back to lead the Muslims for a period before the Day of Judgement.

Many Sunnis also believe in the 12 'Imams' as pious Muslims of high spiritual ranks through their association with the Prophet and the blessing of Allah. However, they:

■ disagree with the exact definition of 'Imam'

- do not believe Imam Mahdi has been born yet

- believe the political or worldly leader of the Muslims should be chosen by a vote among a group of pious Muslims and doesn't need to be a descendant of the Prophet (peace be upon him).

The Salafi sect

- The Salafi sect, sometimes also called the Wahhabi sect, emerged about 250 years ago. This is a Sunni sect who believe:

- Muslims have moved away from the true religion of Islam as taught by the Prophet (peace be upon him) and practiced by his companions and the early Muslims (the 'Salaf' - may Allah be pleased with them all).

- A lot of new things (innovations) have been introduced to the religion, which are Haram (such as asking pious people and the Awliyah Allah to pray for you, visiting the graves of Saints, or celebrating the birth of the Prophet – peace be upon him).

- Other Muslims follow a lot of Hadith which are forgeries and their own interpretation of the Qur'an is more literal.

Sufism

Many non-Muslims and even some Muslims believe Sufism is a sect of Islam, however it is more accurate to say that Sufism is a facet of Islam. To be a Sufi is to practice Tasawwuf. This is the part of Islam concerned with purifying your outer and inner self, to bring yourself closer to Allah, to get to know Him, to experience Him. The Prophet taught his companions (may Allah be pleased with them all) how to do this when describing Ihsan (excellence in worship):

"...It is that you should serve Allah as though you could see Him, for though you cannot see Him yet (know that) He sees you." (Muslim)

And in another famous Hadith Kudsi:

Verily Allah has said: 'Whosoever shows enmity to a Wali (friend) of Mine, then I have declared war against him. And My servant does not draw near to Me with anything

more beloved to Me than the religious duties I have obligated upon him. And My servant continues to draw near to me with Nawafil (supererogatory) deeds until I love him. When I love him, I become his hearing with which he hears, his sight with which he sees, his hand with which he strikes, and his foot with which he walks. Were he to ask [something] of Me, I would surely give it to him; and were he to seek refuge with Me, I would surely grant him refuge.' **(Bukhari)**

Followers of Sufism still believe one must follow commandments within the Qur'an and the example of the Prophet (peace be upon him) in order to practice Islam. Some people claim to be Sufis but do not adhere to the basic tenets of the faith, claiming to have been granted an exemption by Allah, or having been allowed to do things otherwise considered Haram. These are people who are following their Nafs (ego, or desires), they are not Sufis.

Muslims who want to practice Tasawwuf try and find a teacher, a Murshid (one of the Awliyah-Allah), and become their student (Mureed). Genuine chains of these students and teachers can be traced all the way back to the Prophet Muhammad (peace be upon him) and his family and companions (may Allah be pleased with them all). These chains belong to different 'schools' or 'orders', named after famous Awliyah Allah, including Qadiri, Naqshbandi, Chisti, Suhrawardi, Shadhili, etc.

Madhab – schools of religious law

There is often confusion between sects and Madhab (schools of religious law). From the Qur'an and Hadith of the Prophet (peace be upon him) scholars have extracted rules and laws, collectively called the Shariah. Scholars study the Shariah (the subject is called Fiqh), to explain it to common Muslims and to apply it to different circumstances and issues not contemporary to the time of the Prophet (peace be upon him). To do this they have to understand why Allah and the Prophet (peace be upon him) told us to do things in a certain way.

For example, ordinarily we are required to fast from Sunrise to Sunset. However now there are Muslims living in countries so far north or south that their days or nights can last longer than 24 hours.

Similarly, Muslims pray facing the Ka'bah in Makkah but what about someone on an aeroplane or a Muslim astronaut on board a spaceship? How can Muslims know the answers to these questions when these things did not occur during the time of the Prophet (peace be upon him)?

Mujtahid

The Islamic scholars who create these rulings based on the Qur'an and Hadith are called Mujtahid. They are people who have spent their lives studying Islam. The collection of their rulings is called a 'school of religious law', or Madhab. Different Mujtahid can have differences in opinion (based on their understanding of what the Qur'an and Hadith is telling us and why), giving rise to different Islamic rulings. But this does not mean one is right and the other is wrong; the famous Mujtahid in the past from whom we have the different Madhab all loved and respected each other even when they disagreed. Out of this respect, if they visited each other they would act according to the Islamic rulings of their host.

So within the different sects of Islam there can be different Madhab. In Sunni these are called Hanafi, Maliki, Shafi, and Hanbali after the famous Mujtahid Imam Abu Hanifa, Imam Malik, Imam Shafi, and Imam Ahmad ibn Hanbal (may Allah have mercy upon them all).

Conclusion

The Prophet (peace be upon him) told us just as religions before us had sects, so would the Muslims. Unfortunately, instead of focussing on the vast majority of common beliefs we all share, and loving and helping each other as the creation of Allah and followers of the Prophet (peace be upon him), we focus on the small differences between us, and let this develop into a hatred for our brothers and sisters in Islam, to the extent that we even fight and kill each other. Allah told us in the Qur'an to remove hatred from our hearts for fellow Muslims, and the Prophet (peace be upon him) told us that when Muslims fight, both are destined for Hell.

"Our Lord, forgive us and our brothers in faith who passed away, and don't leave any hatred in our hearts for the believers..." (Qur'an 59:10)

The Prophet (peace be upon him) said: "A Muslim is a brother to a Muslim. He should neither deceive him nor lie to him, nor leave him without assistance. Everything belonging to a Muslim is inviolable for a Muslim; his honour, his blood and property. Piety is here (and he pointed out to his chest thrice). It is enough for a Muslim to commit evil by despising his Muslim brother." (Tirmidhi)

The Prophet (peace be upon him) said: "If two Muslims confront each other with swords, both the killer and the killed will be in Hellfire." It was said, "O Messenger of Allah, we understand for the killer, but why for the one killed?" The Prophet said, "Verily, he intended to kill his companion." (Bukhari)

Imagine, that if the Prophet (peace be upon him) showed love and kindness even to his worst enemies, how should we behave towards other Muslims regardless of what they believe? The Prophet (peace be upon him) told stories to his companions of how even kindness to animals can please Allah enough for Him to forgive major sins. If being kind to an animal can earn the pleasure of Allah, imagine how He would reward someone who is kind to their Muslim brothers and sisters?

The Prophet (peace be upon him) said: "A prostitute had once been forgiven. She passed by a dog panting near a well. Thirst had nearly killed him, so she took off her sock, tied it to her veil, and drew up some water. Allah forgave her for that." (Muslim)

Questions

- Why do religions split into sects?

- What are the names of the two major sects in Islam, and why did they branch off?

- Why is the Ahmadiyya movement not considered a sect of Islam?

- Why is Sufism not considered a sect of Islam?

- What is a Madhab?

- Why are Madhabs important, why can't we just read the Qur'an and Hadith to find out what we should do?

- How should Muslims of different sects behave with each other?

Activities

- Find out from your Muslim friends what sect of Islam their family belongs to. Do you feel any differently about them after finding this out, and why?

- Talk to your friends about the similarities and differences between these sects

- Do some research regarding the many different subjects Islamic scholars study to understand the Qur'an and Hadith so they can make religious rulings, and how many years of study it takes before they are qualified to do this

- Find out from your parents, relatives or a friend of the family if they are a student in a Sufi order, and what kind of things their teacher teaches them

- If you see someone being bullied because of their sect, stand up for them

1 . 5

The Death Penalty and Hudud Punishments

Objectives

- To understand how criminals are punished according to Shariah law

- To explore the different crimes that qualify for Hudud punishments

- To consider the historical context of how these punishments were enforced

Keywords

- Shariah

- Tazir

- Qisas

- Hudud

A complete way of life

Islam is not just a religion, but a complete way of life. Using the Qur'an and Sunnah of the Prophet (peace be upon him), religious scholars have described the Shariah for every part of our life from the cradle to the grave. It is a great blessing of Allah that He has given us these laws; just as a teacher tells their students they are going to have a test and then provides them with the answers. What excuse do they then have if they fail? In the same way, Allah has made it easy for us to live our life in a way that will please Him, for which He will reward us with eternal life in His Paradise.

Punishments for crimes in Shariah law

The Shariah contains laws regarding different criminal punishments. These are split into three, Tazir, Qisas, and Hudud. Tazir means the judge will decide what punishment to give the criminal. This is for crimes that do not fit under the other two categories.

Qisas means retaliation, it is where the punishment matches the crime. So if a criminal is guilty of murder, they are given the death penalty. Or if a criminal is guilty of beating someone up which caused them to lose sight in one of their eyes, the criminal would also lose an eye. Qisas also applies to property damage.

Believers, retribution is prescribed for you in the case of victims of murderers: a free man for a free man, a slave for a slave, and a woman for a woman... (Qur'an 2:178)

In the Torah We commanded: a life for a life; an eye for an eye; a nose for a nose; an ear for an ear; a tooth for a tooth; all injuries like for like. (Qur'an 5:45)

Narrated Syedina Anas (may Allah be pleased with him): "The daughter of An-Nadr slapped a girl and broke her incisor tooth. They (the relatives of that girl), came to the Prophet (peace be upon him) and he gave the order of Qisas." (Bukhari)

One of the wisdoms in having this sort of punishment is that the victim and their family will be satisfied that justice has been done. It also acts as a deterrent, since the criminal planning such a crime will know that if they are caught they will receive a similarly severe punishment, and will be less likely to go ahead with it. As murderers are killed, it also stops them from murdering again, whereas a punishment such as temporary imprisonment does not remove this possibility.

In this way, Islam protects the rights of people against whom crimes are committed, but it is also a religion of mercy and kindness. In the Qur'an Allah tells us that if someone commits a crime against us, it is our right to ask for Qisas but there is also an option to take a certain amount of money from the criminal in compensation instead, and spare them the punishment they would otherwise have received.

...However, if the culprit is pardoned by his aggrieved brother, this will be adhered to in accordance with best practice, the culprit paying the next of kin what is due. This represents a lightening of the burden and an act of kindness from your Lord... (Qur'an 2:178)

This is called Diyah, and Allah describes it as a mercy for the believers. The Prophet (peace be upon him) told us that if we really want to make Allah happy and get closer to him, we can go further and just forgive the criminal as an act of charity.

...Whoever gives up his right out of charity, that will serve as an atonement for him on Judgement Day... (Qur'an 5:45)

Hudud crimes and punishments

Hudud means boundaries or limits. These punishments are for crimes that go against the limits or boundaries set by Allah, as described in the Qur'an or Hadith of the Prophet (peace be upon him). Hudud crimes include stealing something valuable, highway robbery (stealing with violence or murder), fornication or adultery (having sex before marriage, or with someone other than your husband or wife), accusing someone of fornication or adultery without proof, drinking alcohol, war against Allah, and spreading corruption on Earth.

The last two includes becoming an enemy of the Muslim state (treason), especially if someone used to be a Muslim and then converts to a different religion. This is called apostasy, but it is not the same as someone changing their religion in this day and age, it has to be understood by how societies worked at the time of the Prophet (peace be upon him). At that time, community was based on religion rather than country or race, so if someone left one religion and joined another it was as if they were changing sides in a war and working for the enemy. So the Hudud crime here was not in purely leaving Islam, but leaving Islam and working against the religion. Allah tells us in the Qur'an that there is no compulsion in religion, that no-one can be forced to accept Islam:

There is no compulsion in religion. Guidance is clearly distinct from error. (Qur'an 2:256)

If an Islamic state in this day and age (when community is no longer based on religion) was to punish people who left Islam by killing them, that would be the same as forcing them to remain as Muslims even if they didn't want to.

The punishments for Hudud crimes include death by stoning, whipping, crucifixion, amputation of the hand, and cutting off of the hands and feet.

The penalty for thieves, male and female, is to cut off their hands, a deterrent from Allah... (Qur'an 5:38)

The proper punishment for those who start war to destroy the people of Allah and His Messenger is: the death penalty, or crucifixion, or amputation of their hands and feet on opposite sides, or be exiled from the city... (Qur'an 5:33)

Flog the fornicators, male and female, each of them one-hundred lashes, and don't let sympathy for them hold you back from fulfilling Allah's orders... (Qur'an 24:2)

Why such severe punishments?

What these crimes have in common is that they aaffect the whole of the Muslim community. If they are not stopped they will spread, becoming more common, eventually causing the whole community to move away from Islam, from morality and good character without which civilised society breaks down.

They will also lead to other problems. For example, a small proportion of people are unable to moderate the amount of alcohol they drink. When they are drunk they become argumentative and violent, losing the ability to take care of themselves and having to go to hospital. This wastes the time of paramedics,

doctors and nurses. If they regularly drink in excess they will permanently damage their health and become significantly unwell, again taking up the time of doctors and nurses, and money that hospitals could be spending taking care of other sick people. Similarly, people who commit adultery cause families to break apart and fornication leads to high rates of teenage pregnancies. By specifically mentioning these crimes, Allah is telling us how important it is to refrain from them. The severe punishments also act as a deterrent.

The burden of evidence

At the time of the Prophet (peace be upon him) and the early Muslims (may Allah be pleased with them all), the punishments for Hudud crimes were hardly ever carried out, even on obtaining a confession.

Firstly, this is because Allah has set the bar of evidence very high for proving that a Hudud crime has taken place. For example, if two people were found naked in bed we would assume they have had sex, but for it to be proved according to Islamic law four people would need to have seen them engaged in the sexual act for them to be found guilty. Even if someone confessed to one of these crimes, all they had to do was later retract their confession to escape punishment.

The Prophet (peace be upon him) encouraged people to forgive each other and hide their sins (obviously having done Istighfar and making the intention to never do them again)..

The Prophet (peace be upon him) said: "All of my Ummah will be forgiven except those who sin openly. It is a part of sinning openly when a man does something at night, then the following morning when Allah has concealed his sin, he says, 'O So and so, I did such and such last night,' when all night his Lord has concealed him and the next morning he uncovers what Allah had concealed." (Bukhari)

The Prophet (peace be upon him) said: "Whoever removes a worldly hardship from a believer, Allah will remove one of the hardships of the Day of Resurrection from him. Whoever grants respite to (a debtor) who is in difficulty, Allah will grant him relief in this world and in the Hereafter. Whoever conceals (the fault of) a Muslim in this world, Allah will conceal him (his faults) in this world and in the Hereafter. Allah will help a person so long as he is helping his brother." (Muslim)

The Prophet (peace be upon him) said: "Overlook mistakes committed by people of good character." (Abu Dawood)

The judge should also try to find any sort of excuse to not apply the Hudud punishments. For example, if someone stole something and was witnessed by two people, as required for the Hudud punishment, if the thief claimed the item to be his that would be enough to stop him from having his hand amputated. Similarly, if someone's breath was found smelling of alcohol that would not be enough evidence of having actually consumed alcohol for the Hudud punishment. Even if someone was drunk and vomited up wine this would not be sufficient evidence because they could have drunk it by mistake.

The Prophet (peace be upon him) told us it is better for a judge to make a mistake and let a criminal go, then to make a mistake and punish an innocent person.

The Prophet (peace be upon him) said, "Avoid applying legal punishments against the Muslims if you are able. If the criminal has a way out, then leave him to his way. Verily, for the leader to err in pardoning is better than to err in punishing." (Tirmidhi)

But just because the Hudud punishment is not used for a crime, it does not mean the criminal receives no punishment at all. The judge decides, based on the crime committed, what is a fitting punishment (Tazir).

Why Muslims would confess

The few times when punishments for Hudud crimes were carried out during the lifetime of the Prophet (peace be upon him) and early Muslims (may Allah be pleased with them all) was when the criminal would confess, and couldn't be convinced to retract their confession.

Why would someone do this? It is because these people understood that by doing Istighfar and then receiving punishment for their crime in this life, it will save them from punishment in the grave, on the Day of Judgement and in Hell. No matter how painful the punishment you receive in this life, it is nothing compared to the punishment of the afterlife. In Tafsir ibn Kathir, he includes a Hadith from Musnad Abu Ya'la, in which a man came to the Prophet (peace be upon him) and confessed to committing fornication. The Prophet (peace be upon him) turned his face from him as if he had not heard him, but the man kept confessing until the Prophet asked him what he wanted. The man said he wanted to be purified.

So the Prophet (peace be upon him) ordered for him to be stoned to death. After he had died the Prophet overheard some of his companions (may Allah be pleased with them all) saying that Allah had hidden this man's sin but he chose to reveal it and was stoned to death. The Prophet (peace be upon him) told them off for backbiting about their Muslim brother and told them that their brother was swimming in the rivers of Paradise.

Vigilante justice

An important point to make is that any sort of punishment under Shariah can only be carried out by the judiciary or legal system, never by a group of people or a single person. If anyone other than the judiciary were to take justice into their own hands, no matter how certain they were of the crime, they would be punished since their actions are considered criminal according to Shariah. This means that if Muslims live in a country that has a different system of laws, they are meant to live by the laws of the land, not try and implement Shariah by themselves.

Believers, obey Allah, the Messenger and those among you in authority... (Qur'an 4:59)

The Prophet (peace be upon him) said: "It is necessary upon a Muslim to listen to and obey the ruler, as long as one is not ordered to carry out a sin. If he is commanded to commit a sin, then there is no adherence and obedience." (Bukhari)

Conclusion

If we live our life according to the rules Allah has revealed to us this will lead to peace and happiness, for the individual and the whole community both in this life and the next. In the Shariah there are some very severe punishments, but they are for crimes that would harm the wider community if they were allowed to spread. However, Allah's mercy is such that these punishments are meant to serve as a deterrent, a reminder of Allah's intense displeasure, and any excuse is found to not apply them. Even when they are put into practice it is still a blessing from Allah, since it will mean we pay for our sins in this life and avoid punishment in the hereafter.

Questions

- What is Shariah?

- What are the three types of laws regarding punishments in Islam?

- What are the three possible outcomes of Qisas?

- What are the Hudud crimes, why are they called that, and what do they have in common?

- What are the punishments for Hudud crimes, and what is their purpose?

- How can such severe punishments be considered a blessing from Allah?

Activities

- Visit a Shariah court and talk to the judge about how they decide on what punishments to give

- Do some research regarding when imprisonment became the normal method of punishment for most serious crimes in the Western world, and what they used to do before this

- Do some research regarding which countries in the world still use capital punishment, and the methods they use

1 . 6

Jihad

Objectives

- To understand the concept of Jihad in Islam

- To explore the different ways a Muslim can engage in Jihad

- To consider the need for rules of engagement when performing Jihad to free people from oppression

Keywords

- Jihad

- Nafs

- Dawah

- Oppression

The literal translation

There is a common misconception in the world today that the Islamic concept of 'Jihad' is synonymous with violence, murdering of non-Muslim 'infidels', suicide bombings and beheadings. Jihad is an Arabic word and is derived from the trilateral verb 'Ja-Ha-Da' which means 'to strive', or 'struggle'. In this chapter we will discuss some of the different forms of Jihad described within the Qur'an and Hadith of the Prophet (peace be upon him).

Jihad against yourself

The first and foremost Jihad all Muslims should be engaged in is against their own self. Our Nafs is our ego, or the animalistic part of our self that encourages us to indulge in worldly and bodily pleasures. It is what makes us greedy, to want more than we need, and to be envious of what others have even when we have plenty. It is what makes us spend our time and effort hording wealth and possessions and showing them off to others around us. It encourages us to engage in shameful behaviour and seek out bodily pleasures, whether by looking at pornography and masturbating, fornicating or committing adultery. And when something makes us angry, when we believe someone has slighted us, it is what makes us lose control of ourselves, sometimes to the extent of causing others bodily harm or even death, let alone the hurt we cause by the unrestrained use of our tongues.

The Nafs does not care about right or wrong, about Halal or Haram. Therefore, if we were to spend our life following its desires we would be no better than animals.

And so it is that many of the Jinn and humans that We've created are intended for Hell. They have brains which don't think, eyes that don't see, and ears that don't hear, such people are like cattle, even more dumb, worse than them; they are unaware of reality. (Qur'an 7:179)

As Muslims, living our lives according to the boundaries set by Allah in the Qur'an and Sunnah of the Prophet (peace be upon him) necessarily involves struggling against the desires of our Nafs, i.e. performing Jihad against ourselves. In a widely quoted weak Hadith, the Prophet (peace be upon him) told his companions, on return from the battlefield, "Congratulations on your safe return, you have returned from a lesser battlefield to a greater battle. The greater battle for a man is to fight against his lowly desires."

This message is strengthened by many other Hadith and the Qur'an itself. The Prophet (peace be upon him) said in his farewell pilgrimage, "...The Mujahid (one who engages in Jihad) is he who makes Jihad against himself ('Jahada Nafsah') for the sake of obeying Allah." (Tirmidhi)

In another Hadith he said, "The strong are not the best wrestlers. Verily, the strong are only those who control themselves when they are angry." (Bukhari)

And in the Qur'an, Allah tells us:

By the human He made perfect; so inspired him to follow either its vice or virtue. Whoever purified himself succeeded, and whoever was immoral failed himself. (Qur'an 91:7-10)

But the one who feared standing before His Lord and stopped himself from following his lusts, he will be at home, in Paradise. (Qur'an 79:40-41)

This Jihad includes restraining ourselves from committing sins and also pushing ourselves to not only fulfil the obligatory aspects of our faith, but constantly striving to improve our character, help those around us, and increase our 'Taqwa' (consciousness of Allah), all through following the example of the Prophet (peace be upon him). In this way, every action performed with the intention of seeking the pleasure of Allah is part of this Jihad.

A group of women once came to the Prophet (peace be upon him) and asked to be allowed to take part in a battle. He said to them "Pilgrimage is your Jihad." (Bukhari)

Similarly, a man came to the Prophet (peace be upon him) seeking permission to take part in a battle. The Prophet (peace be upon him) asked the man if his parents were alive, to which he replied that they were. The Prophet (peace be upon him) told him, "Go and serve them, that's your Jihad." (Muslim)

One day the Prophet (peace be upon him) said to his companions (may Allah be pleased with them all), "Shall I tell you something that is the best of all deeds,

constitutes the best act of piety in the eyes of your Lord, elevates your rank in the Hereafter, and carries more virtue than the spending of gold and silver in the service of Allah, or taking part in Jihad and slaying or being slain in the path of Allah?" The companions said: "Yes!" He said: "Remembrance of Allah." (Ahmad)

Some companions of the Prophet (peace be upon him) said to him: "O Messenger of Allah, the rich people will get more reward. They pray as we pray, and they fast as we fast, but they give in charity from their excess wealth." The Prophet (peace be upon him) said, "Has not Allah given you things with which you can give charity? Every Tasbeehah (saying 'Subhaan Allah - Glory

Islam, from ancient times to the modern day

be to Allah') is a charity. Every Takbeerah (saying 'Allahu akbar - Allah is Most Great') is a charity. Every Tahmeedah (saying 'Al-Hamdu-Lillah - praise be to Allah)' is a charity. Every Tahleelah (saying 'Laa illaha ill-Allah - there is no god but Allah') is a charity. Enjoining what is good is a charity. Forbidding what is evil is a charity. Having intercourse (with one's wife) is a charity." The companions (may Allah be pleased with them all) said, "O Messenger of Allah, if one of us fulfils his desire, is there reward in that?" He replied, "Do you not see that if he does it in a Haram way he will have the burden of sin? So if he does it in a Halal way, he will have a reward for that." (Muslim)

Dawah – spreading the message of Islam

If we spend our time engaged in Jihad against our Nafs, it will eventually and inevitably result in an improvement in our character and behaviour with others, be they Muslims or non-Muslims, family or friends, at school or at work. Indeed, the character of everyday, ordinary Muslim men and women is the single most powerful tool for Dawah that they possess. When non-Muslims see the excellent character of true Muslims they interact with in their daily lives, they will notice a pattern, their curiosity will be piqued and

they will want to find out what it is about this religion that makes its followers behave in this way.

They will learn, through their own research or conversations with Muslims that their good behaviour is because they are following the example of the gentlest and kindest human being to have ever lived, the Prophet of Islam (peace be upon him), as Allah instructs us in the Qur'an.

By the grace of your Lord, Prophet, you aren't possessed. Indeed, you shall have an everlasting reward, and you have a strong character. (Qur'an 68:2-4)

You have an excellent role model in the Messenger of Allah, particularly for anyone who longs for Allah and the Last Day and remembers Him abundantly. (Qur'an 33:21)

The Prophet (peace be upon him) said, "Nothing is weightier on the Scale of Deeds than one's good manners. Verily, Allah hates the vulgar, obscene person." (Tirmidhi)

The Prophet (peace be upon him) said, "I was sent to perfect good character." (Al Albani)

It is through the merciful and loving nature of the Prophet (peace be upon him) that many of even his staunchest enemies, who had engaged in fighting again, torturing and killing Muslims, eventually came to accept Islam and became devout Muslims.

Due to the kindness you have been granted from Allah, you were lenient with them; had you been harsh and hard-hearted they would have deserted you, so pardon, seek forgiveness and consult them. (Qur'an 3:159)

As we see in the stories of the battle of Uhud, Ta'if and the conquest of Mecca, even when the Prophet (peace be upon him) was in a position of power, able to punish those who had wronged him and his companions, his character was such that he instead chose to forgive and pray for them.

We sent you, Muhammad, as kindness for all communities. (Qur'an 21:107)

It is incumbent upon all Muslims to do our part in spreading the true message of Islam, within our sphere of influence, to those who have not yet received it. We will fulfil this by performing Jihad to try and emulate the character of the Prophet (peace be upon him), and to not shy away from telling others of our faith in a friendly and inviting manner without being preachy and confrontational. This will help reduce Islamophobia (fear of Islam and Muslims based on ignorance) and if Allah wills, someone we know may even accept Islam and become Muslim.

Whose speech can be better than the one who calls to Allah and acts righteously and states openly: "I am a Muslim." (Qur'an 41:33)

Educating yourself about your faith

But what are we to do if non-Muslims see our good character and wishing to know more about Islam, start asking us questions? Unfortunately, the majority of us would not be able to provide suitable answers to even some of the most basic questions about our faith. This leads us onto another form of Jihad, which is to educate ourselves about the fundamentals of Islam, which is also incumbent upon every Muslim. Not only will this allow us to practice our religion properly, but we will also be able to speak confidently about our faith.

The Prophet (peace be upon him) said, "Seeking knowledge is a duty upon every Muslim..." (Ibn Majah)

The Prophet (peace be upon him) said, "The best of charity is when a Muslim man gains knowledge, then he teaches it to his Muslim brother." (Ibn Majah)

The Prophet (peace be upon him) said, "The best of you are those who learn the Qur'an and teach it." (Bukhari)

The Prophet (peace be upon him) said, "Whoever teaches some knowledge will have the reward of the one who acts upon it, without that detracting from his reward in the slightest." (Ibn Majah)

The Prophet (peace be upon him) said, "One Faqih (knowledgeable man) is more formidable against the Shaitan than one thousand devoted worshipers." (Ibn Majah)

Invite to your Lord's way wisely; teaching in a pleasant manner, and debating with courtesy... (Qur'an 16:125)

There should always be a group among you that calls people to what is best, enjoins the common good and forbids evil; this group of people are the successful. (Qur'an 3:104)

Indeed, this was the form of Jihad all Prophets were engaged in for the entirety of their Prophethoods.

So this Jihad requires us to learn more about Islam, and how fortunate are we that in today's day and age this is so easy, especially in the UK with the sheer number of mosques, there are regular Islamic circles and weekly gatherings that can be attended, not to mention Jumma speeches, and no shortage of Islamic bookshops. There are also several Islamic TV/internet channels and radio stations/podcasts.

Spending our wealth to support the community

Most of these services are available to us for free, but they are not free to provide. This leads to another form of Jihad, which is to spend the wealth that Allah has blessed us with to not only help others less fortunate than ourselves, but to also support educational services and projects.

Indeed, true believers are those who believed in Allah and His Messenger, and had no doubts. They strived with their wealth and their lives in Allah's way. (Qur'an 49:15)

Those who believed, migrated and struggled in Allah's way with their wealth and lives have a special place near Allah; these are the real winners. (Qur'an 9:20)

However, the Messenger and believers strive with their wealth and lives. They shall have all the best things, and they're successful. (Qur'an 9:88)

In all three of these Qur'anic verses the word 'Jahadu' (the verb for Jihad) is being used to describe spending wealth in the way of Allah. It is our duty, as the Muslim community, to help support initiatives which aim to spread the message of Islam to non-Muslims, and better educate Muslims about their religion. By doing so we are taking part in a form of 'Sadaqa Jariya' – ongoing charity, which has the potential to benefit us even after our death.

The Prophet (peace be upon him) said, "When a person dies, all their deeds end except three: a continuing charity, beneficial knowledge and a child who prays for them." (Muslim)

Freeing our fellow human beings from oppression

But there are times when the help our fellow human beings need from us is to free them from oppression. This brings us to the most widely recognised form of Jihad. However, even this can take many forms, from legal, diplomatic and economic, to political means. But if there is no peaceful alternative, Islam does allow the use of force.

Fight in Allah's way those who fight you, but do not attack first. Allah does not like the aggressors. (Qur'an 2:190)

What is the matter with you that you do not fight in the way or Allah when the weak – mean, women and children – are saying, "Our Lord, out of Your graciousness, take us out of this town of cruel people, give us protectors and helpers!" (Qur'an 4:75)

There are strict preconditions and rules of engagement, it is not a matter of any Muslim individual or group being able to declare Jihad as they wish, and upon whomever they wish, and with no regard for the collateral damage they cause, killing innocent men, women and children in the process. And this type of help is very specifically not a religious war waged against those of other faiths; it is clearly stated in the Qur'an that "There is no compulsion in religion." (Qur'an 2:256)

Islam does not consider the taking of a human life as an insignificant act, it is only permissible under the most extreme of circumstances. Allah says in the Qur'an, "Whoever kills a person, except as a punishment for murder or mischief in the land, it will be

written in his book of deeds as if he had killed all the human beings on the surface of the Earth..." (Qur'an 5:32)

Even when a just war is fought by a state or country, the behaviour of Muslims must be in accordance with the high standards Allah and His Prophet (peace be upon him) expect, even on the battlefield.

The Prophet (peace be upon him) said, "Do not kill the people who are sitting in places of worship." (Ibn Hanbal)

The Prophet (peace be upon him) said, "Do not kill any child, any woman, or any elderly or sick person." (Abu Dawud)

During a war, the Prophet (peace be upon him) saw a corpse of a woman lying on the ground and observed: "She was not fighting, how then did she come to be killed?"

The Prophet (peace be upon him) said, "Do not practice treachery or mutilation. Do not uproot or burn palms or cut down fruitful trees. Do not slaughter a sheep or a cow or a camel, except for food." (Al-Muwatta)

The Prophet (peace be upon him) said, "Do not destroy the villages and towns, do not spoil the cultivated fields and gardens, and do not slaughter the cattle." (Bukhari)

Fight them until there is no more persecution, and people are free to worship Allah. If they cease fighting, then let there be no more hostility except against wrongdoers. (Qur'an 2:193)

This is especially important regarding prisoners of war, which the Prophet (peace be upon him) advised his companions to treat in a humane manner. This included favouring them over themselves when it came to clothing and feeding, not forcing them to change their religion, and not separating prisoners from the same family.

They fulfil their vows, fear a Day whose horror will be widespread, they feed the needy, the orphan and the prisoner for the love of Allah, saying, "We feed you for His sake; we don't want some payment or thanks from you." (Qur'an 76:7-9)

Syedina Abu Bakr (may Allah be pleased with him), during his reign as the first Caliph of the Muslims, summarised these instructions for his army before a military campaign: "Stop, O people, that I may give you ten rules for your guidance in the battlefield. Do not commit treachery or deviate from the right path. You must not mutilate dead bodies. Neither kill a child, nor a woman, nor an aged man. Bring no harm to the trees, nor burn them with fire, especially those which are fruitful. Slay not any of the enemy's flock, save for your food. You are likely to pass by people who have devoted their lives to monastic services; leave them alone."

The Prophet (peace be upon him) said, "Verily, Allah will torture those who torture people in this world." (Muslim)

Fulfilling all of these conditions, for those who take part in this Jihad and sacrifice their life to free their fellow human beings from oppression, Allah bestows upon them great rewards.

And we must be careful to not become the aggressors, seeking vengeance.

Those killed in Allah's way, don't consider them dead; rather they're alive, being provided for in the presence of their Lord. (Qur'an 3:169)

When the Prophet (peace be upon him) was asked about this verse, he explained to his companions (may Allah be pleased with them all), "Their souls will live inside green birds that dwell in designated lamps which hang on the throne of Allah, they will roam freely in Paradise as they please, then return to these lamps." (Muslim)

And in another Prophetic Hadith, he told us, "Nobody who enters Paradise would ever wish to return to this life again, even if he was to be given the whole world and everything in it – except for a martyr; for he would wish to return and get killed ten times due to the honour that he received (in Paradise)." (Bukhari)

Conclusion

Jihad should not be mistranslated as 'holy war'. When we understand the true meaning of the word and the concepts it describes, we realise that all of us are involved in Jihad in many different areas of our lives. In fact, it would not be possible to be a true Muslim, or a good human being, without engaging in this constant struggle to improve ourselves and help those around us.

Questions

- What is the meaning of the word Jihad?

- What are the different ways in which we can perform Jihad?

- Does Islam allow the use of violence, and if so, under what circumstances and under which conditions?

Activities

- Make a list of the different ways in which you perform Jihad

- Read about any recent terrorist attacks that have taken place, and consider whether they would fulfil the criteria to be classified as Jihad

Islam, from ancient times to the modern day

1 . 7

Riba

Objectives

- To understand why Riba is not permitted in Islam

- To explore the different forms Riba can take in the modern world

- To consider how Muslims can live in countries with economies based on interest

Keywords

- Riba

- Interest

- Loan

- Banking

Riba versus charity

Allah forbids Muslims from giving or taking Riba. In the Qur'an He contrasts it with charity and how money made using Riba will have no benefit in it whereas He will multiply the rewards for money spent in charity. He warns the believers to fear Him and give up their desire for Riba if they want to be successful. He threatens us, that if we do not take notice of this warning then Allah and His Prophet (peace be upon him) will go to war with us.

The wealth you lend people with interest for an increase will not increase in Allah's sight; but what you give in Zakat, seeking Allah's pleasure will increase, such people will be rewarded many times over. (Qur'an 30:39)

Believers, be mindful of Allah and give up any outstanding usury on debts owed to you, if you are true believers. If you do not do so, then heed this declaration of war from Allah and His Messenger... (Qur'an 2:278-279)

What is Riba?

Riba is usually translated as interest and most commonly is used to mean giving a loan where the person has to pay back more than the amount they borrowed, whether all at once or over time. It can also involve exchange of goods, where they are of different value.

Some scholars argue that Allah has forbidden interest because it corrupts the purpose of money, which is to be able to buy and sell and exchange different types of goods. Interest allows you to make more money just using the money you already have, without any kind of buying and selling, without any effort or hard work, and without any risk. This encourages hoarding of wealth and not spending it, and increases the gap between the rich and poor in society. But scholars disagree about whether Allah's warning to the Muslims regarding Riba includes all, or only some forms of interest, given that in the world we live in today nearly all types of financial transactions include interest.

Riba at the time of the Prophet (peace be upon him)

Some scholars argue that Riba includes all forms of interest, including mortgages to buy houses and bank loans that are taken out by people, businesses, and even countries. It would also include the interest payments banks give to customers on their savings.

Other scholars disagree, arguing that even though these transactions include interest, they should not be included in Riba. They say we need

to consider what constituted Riba at the time of the Prophet (peace be upon him), when these verses of the Qur'an were being revealed. At that time, Riba was when rich people (loan sharks) would lend money to poor people who were in desperate need to buy basic necessities. The money would be lent on condition that twice, three times, or even more, would be paid back on a specific date, and if payment was late it would increase further. This resulted in poor people ending up with large debts to rich people, which would continue increasing over time. This resulted in them effectively becoming slaves for the rest of their lives since they had no way of paying off the huge increasing debt they were under.

Riba in the modern world

We can see some examples of this in the modern world. Loan sharks still exist. But there are even legitimate businesses that advertise themselves as offering payday loans or short term loans. They offer money to people who've run out money before they get their next pay cheque. They purposefully don't carry out the same background checks banks do to see if these people will be able to pay the money back, and then charge huge amounts of interest on late payments.

Compound interest loans also cause similar problems. Normally, interest is charged on a monthly or yearly basis on the principle (the original loan amount). In compound interest, each time interest is charged the principle increases by that amount. This means each time interest is charged, because the principle keeps growing, the interest charged keeps increasing. In this way, the amount of money owed grows larger faster and faster, until the amount of interest being charged is actually more than the initial principle that was borrowed. So some scholars argue that it is these types of unethical and high interest financial transactions that Riba is referring to.

A slippery slope

However, in response to this, some scholars point out that during the time of the Prophet (peace be upon him) there were Arabs who were very wealthy. They would have been involved in giving or taking huge loans and having large business dealings with each other and businessmen from the neighbouring Byzantine empire that would have involved interest.

So Riba, or interest at the time of the Prophet (peace be upon him) did not only involve loan sharks, yet the Qur'anic verses and Hadith quite clearly ban all Riba without making exceptions for the type or amount of interest, or transactions it involves. If you drink a little bit of wine you won't get drunk, in fact there is some research that it is even healthy, but Allah has still prohibited Muslims from drinking any amount of alcohol.

In the same way, small amounts of interest that are regulated by banks who perform checks on the people or businesses they lend money to, to see if they are likely to be able to pay it back, might even be good for the economy and help people who want to buy a house or start a business.

However even some non-Muslims economists agree that there are many problems caused by interest, including high levels of debt for individual people who can end up homeless and bankrupt, but also entire countries whose governments have taken compound interest loans but can't pay it back as fast as the debt is increasing, leading to entire populations suffering for generations. For example, Nigeria borrowed $5 billion up to 1985 and have paid back $16 billion, yet still owe $28 billion due to the rate of compound interest on the initial $5 billion.

A financial system based on interest, combined with a culture of greed and lack of accountability also creates an incentive for loans to be given to people who can't afford to repay them and then buying and selling of such debt between banks and financial institutions. This led to the credit crisis in 2007-2008 which destabilised nearly the entire world's economy.

Therefore, some scholars argue that because interest can cause such severe problems, impacting the lives of millions of people, even if it can do some good, overall it is an evil and so Allah has prohibited it in all its forms. By doing so, this will force us to find alternate ways to engage in financial transactions that are Halal, which we might not do if we accept that some forms of interest are allowed, and don't classify them as Riba.

Islamic banking

Islamic banking was developed In the 20th century and offers an alternative for Muslims who don't want to give or take interest. This mainly involves two types of transaction called Murabahah and Musharakah.

Murabahah involves a charge for buying something on credit. For example, you could buy a car for £20,000 right now, or pay £2,000 every month for a year (therefore totalling £24,000). Musharakah is profit and loss sharing. For example, if someone wants to buy a house for £200,000, they could borrow it from the bank. Until they have repaid this amount, both they and the bank are joint owners of the house. During the period in which they are repaying the loan, if the house increases in value the amount they repay each month to the bank would increase to reflect this (profit sharing), but if the house was to decrease in value, the amount they repay each month to the bank would decrease to reflect this (loss sharing). As they repay more and more of their loan, the share of the house they own increases and the share the bank owns decreases.

Since deposits and savings in Islamic banking do not earn interest, to compete with other banks and attract customers, Islamic banking accounts often offer some sort of reward or prize for its customers (Hibah). Other financial instruments include Sukuk (Islamic bonds) and Takaful (Islamic insurance).

Is it really 'Islamic' banking?

A not uncommon opinion is that most forms of Islamic banking is a copy of standard banking models and financial transactions with ways found to give or take interest but calling it by another name to justify it as Islamic. Because it is usually more expensive for the customer most Muslims do not choose Islamic banking options when opening a bank account, taking a loan, or choosing a mortgage to buy a house.

Critics complain that instead of finding ways to copy and relabel standard banking models, Islamic banking should have focussed on creating new banking models that found sustainable and profitable ways to help small businesses and poorer individuals.

The scholarly debate continues

The debate among scholars and economists on these, and similar issues continues. Should all interest be considered as Riba and so prohibited according to the strong warnings we find in the Qur'an? In which case, given nearly every country in the world has an economy based on interest, how do individuals go about buying a house or starting a business? Are current Islamic banking practices in line with the principles of Shariah (Islamic law), in which case all Muslims should be encouraged to use these. But if current models of Islamic banking are just copies of interest based banking models, a concerted effort is required among scholars and economists to develop truly Islamic alternatives. What about a Muslim working for a bank or financial institute, who is advising people on taking out mortgages and loans which involve paying interest? Is this a permissible job for a Muslim, when selling alcohol or recreational drugs (other prohibited things) is not?

Conclusion

This topic shows how Islamic scholars are continually engaged in debate regarding everyday issues that affect the common Muslim. Healthy debate involves respectful disagreements based on different interpretations of the Qur'an and Hadith, and this is part of the strength of the Islamic tradition.

Questions

- What is Riba, and what does the Qur'an say regarding it?

- Why is Riba prohibited?

- What types of transactions does Islamic banking use?

- How are these similar to and different from normal banking?

Activities

- Do some research regarding how the modern banking and financial system developed

- Do some research regarding the problems associated with an economy based on interest

- Do some research regarding alternatives that economists have put forward, and their positives and negatives

1 . 8

Science, and the Theory of Evolution

Objectives

- To understand how Islam promotes science as our way of understanding the Universe Allah has created

- To explore the meaning of truth and how our understanding of it can change over time

- To consider how the creation of Adam and Eve fits in with the theory of evolution

Keywords

- Evolution

- Adaptation

- Science

- Truth

The theory of evolution

The theory of evolution is a scientific theory that tells us how animal species can change over time (evolve) due to natural selection. The environment an animal lives in affects how likely it is to survive and reproduce (have children and pass on its genes), compared to another animal of the same species that might be less well adapted, less likely to survive and therefore, less likely to reproduce. In this way, over time, the species changes until all its members are better adapted to their environment.

For example, imagine black and white rabbits living in a snowy environment. The white rabbits have better camouflage and so are less likely to be caught by predators. Therefore, they are more likely to survive long enough to have children and pass on their genes for white fur compared to the black rabbits. Over time, the population of white rabbits will increase. This is called survival of the fittest, and describes how animals are in competition. Those that are better adapted to their environment are more likely to survive and pass on the genes for the adaptation, compared to the animals that aren't.

Now imagine that in this environment it is easier for the rabbits with longer snouts and bigger front arms to dig under the snow to find food. The rabbits which have these adaptations are more likely to pass on genes for these adaptations compared to rabbits with shorter snouts and smaller arms. Over time, rabbits in this environment will all have white fur, longer snouts and bigger front arms. These rabbits will look quite different to black rabbits with shorter snouts and smaller front arms that live in the neighbouring area where there isn't snow, and they might now be considered a different species.

This example shows how, over time, as different adaptations accumulate in the survivors of a specific environment, they become different enough from other animals of the same type in a different environment that they can be identified as a different species. In this way, the theory of evolution says all species originally came from a common ancestor, and that over time, in different environments, natural selection caused animals to adapt and eventually (over millions of years), this caused new species to appear, with birds evolving from reptiles and humans from apes.

What is science?

Science is the name of the way in which we look at, measure, and do experiments to find out how things work, from unimaginably huge galaxies that are millions of light years away from us, to subatomic particles that are invisible even to the most powerful microscopes, to living things and how they think, move, eat, sleep, are born and die. It is a blessing of Allah that He has given humans the ability to understand how He created the Universe, and the rules He made by which it works. We discover these rules when we see patterns in the natural world, such as how light bends when it travels from one substance into another, or how gravity causes huge objects to pull things towards them.

Our ability to do science is always improving as we discover new things and do more experiments with better equipment. This means we are always improving our understanding of the world around us. Quite often we realise that the way we used to think things worked, was incorrect and we replace the previous scientific theory with a new one. It is likely that some of the

scientific theories we have today will have been changed or replaced entirely in the future.

For example, the laws of physics that Isaac Newton, a famous 17th century scientist, described about how objects move in relation to each other, were accepted for nearly 200 years. However, in the 19th century, using more advanced equipment and experiments, scientists found that certain observations of the natural world could not be explained by Newtonian physics, especially on the astronomical scale. When Albert Einstein described his theory of general relativity, this addressed the problems with Newtonian physics. Until now, all experiments and observations have supported Einstein's theory, but the theory does not explain the behaviour of subatomic particles, which the later proposed theory of quantum mechanics currently explains.

Islam, from ancient times to the modern day

Early in the 20th century, Edwin Hubble and other scientists discovered that other galaxies are getting further away from our Milky Way galaxy, and the further away they are, the faster they are travelling, i.e. the Universe is expanding at an ever increasing rate. To explain such findings using the theory of general relativity, scientists came to the conclusion that only less than 10% of the mass and energy of the entire Universe can be explained by what we can see and detect, and over 90% must be 'dark' matter and 'dark' energy. Currently, despite ongoing research all over the world, we haven't yet discovered any physical evidence for these things. In the future, we may well have a better understanding of this.

What is truth?

What all of this goes to show is that to believe that science is the truth is not quite so simple. Science is the search for the truth, but our conclusions depend on our interpretations of the observations we make of the natural world, often through experimentation. Over time these change, so the scientific 'truth' (scientific hypotheses currently accepted as the 'truth') of a thousand years ago is very different to the scientific 'truth' of today, which will almost definitely be different from the scientific 'truth' in a thousand years' time.

Muslims believe everything within the Qur'an to be the words of Allah, His speech, and as such, the absolute truth or reality.

...We revealed to you a glorious Book that explains the truth about all things; it is guidance, a kindness and good news for the Muslims. (Qur'an 16:89)

Allah tells us in the Qur'an that the Prophet (peace be upon him) does not speak of his own accord, but what He says is inspired by Allah. This means Muslims also believe that authentic Hadith of the Prophet (peace be upon him) are the absolute truth.

Your companion has neither strayed nor erred; nor does he speak from personal desire. It is a Divine inspiration. (Qur'an 53:2-4)

The focus of the Qur'an and Hadith is on teaching humanity about the nature of Allah, what we should believe in and how we should worship Him, and how we should live our lives and interact with the rest of creation, both individually and as a community.

This Qur'an could not have been invented independently of Allah; rather it confirms what preceded it and is an explanation of that Book in which there is no doubt, which is from the Lord of all the realms. (Qur'an 10:37)

We revealed the Book so you can explain to them what they differed about; it's a guide and a mercy for believers. (Qur'an 16:64)

In the Qur'an, Allah tells us to look at the world around us, to study it and appreciate how powerful and brilliant the One who created it all must be.

He laid out the land with mountains and running rivers, produced fruits in pairs, and covered the day by the darkness of the night. Surely in this are signs for insightful people. There are neighbouring plots, vineyards, fields and palms, growing either in clusters or standing alone; all are fed by the same water, yet some are better to eat than others. Surely, in this are signs for people who understand. (Qur'an 13:3-4)

He created the night and the day for your benefit; the sun, the moon and the stars all follow His command. In that are signs for those who understand. He produced objects of many colours on the Earth for you; in that are signs for those who accept advice. For your benefit He created the sea; from it you get fresh meat to eat, and extract jewellery that you wear. You see the ships sailing over the waves to seek His gifts, so you may be thankful. He placed the mountains firmly on the Earth, so it doesn't shake beneath you, made the rivers and the tracks so you can find your way, and many other signposts, including the stars for guiding the travellers. (Qur'an 16:12-16)

So the Qur'an encourages science and learning, and Muslims have been responsible for many great scientific discoveries in mathematics, chemistry, astronomy, engineering and agriculture. However, the Qur'an is not a book of science, nor are the collections of Hadith.

Even though Muslims believe the Qur'an and authentic Hadith to be the absolute and unchanging truth, what this truth actually is depends on our understanding of the Qur'anic verses and Hadith, and what we believe they are telling us. This can change over time, especially regarding Qur'anic verses which describe the world around us, which are often interpreted using current scientific theories. For example, in the Qur'an Allah tells us how the

Heavens and the Earth were joined up and how He tore them apart and is responsible for expanding the Heavens. In light of current scientific theories, this is taken to reference the Big Bang and on-going expansion of the Universe.

Don't the disbelievers know the heavens and the Earth were joined at one time? We split them apart... (Qur'an 21:30)

The Qur'an describes the light from the Sun and Moon differently, the Sun is described with words that mean it produces its own light, whereas the Moon is described with words that mean it reflects light.

Blessed is He Who placed constellations in the sky, and made brilliant stars, a shining sun and a bright moon. (Qur'an 25:61)

Regarding the Sun, Earth and Moon, the Arabic words used to describe their motion mean moving on a set path that involves coming back to their starting point, which we now interpret as their orbits.

He created night and day, sun and moon, each one moving in its orbit. (Qur'an 21:33)

On Earth, Allah describes the mountains as pegs, holding it steady, and we now know that mountains have deep roots that extend deep into the Earth, and they do act to stabilise the Earth.

We made the mountains on Earth for stability, so it does not shake beneath them... (Qur'an 21:31)

Allah describes how He made all life on Earth from water.

...and made every living thing from water; won't they believe? (Qur'an 21:30)

Within the womb of a mother, the Qur'an describes different stages of embryonic development:

...We placed him as a drop of semen in the stable environment of the womb. The drop of semen turned to a bloodlike clot; and, from the bloodlike clot, We created a fleshy lump; and then We made bones and covered them with flesh; then We produce from it another created form. Blessed is Allah, the best Creator. (Qur'an 23:12-14)

Islam and the theory of evolution

There is nothing in the Qur'an or Hadith that contradicts natural selection or the evolution of one species from another. But the Qur'an and Hadith of the Prophet (peace be upon him) tell us how Allah created Syedina Adam from clay, before blowing his soul into him, and how from Syedina Adam He created his wife, Syedatuna Hawa (peace be upon them both).

Remember when your Lord said to the Angels, "I am creating a human being from clay. So once I have formed him and blown my spirit into him, prostrate before him." (Qur'an 38:71-72)

People, be mindful of your Lord, He created you from a single person and created his partner from him, and then from the pair He spread countless men and women throughout the world... (Qur'an 4:1)

They are described as the first humans, who initially lived in Paradise before being sent to the Earth, and all of humanity is from their descendants.

We said: "Adam, live with your wife in Paradise and eat freely from wherever you want, but do not go near this tree, or you will be wrongdoers." But Satan tempted them and had them expelled from where they were. We told them:

"Go down as enemies of each other on Earth, you will have a place to live and things to enjoy for a fixed term." (Qur'an 2:35-36)

So how can a Muslim believe in this and the theory of evolution, in which humans are said to evolve from apes?

There is no simple answer to this question. But if it ever seems there is a contradiction between the Qur'an or Hadith and science, it means either our current understanding of the science is incorrect or incomplete, or that our understanding of the Qur'an or Hadith is incorrect or incomplete. Currently, perhaps the easiest way to marry the two is to say that evolution was the system created by Allah which explains all the diversity of life we see on the planet today and that existed long before there were humans on Earth,

leaving behind fossils for us to discover. But when it comes to humans they did not evolve from apes and are a unique creation of Allah.

In fact, humans are not subject to evolution because our survival is not based on adaptation to our environment. Among all of Allah's creation we are unique; He has made us capable of changing our environment and through medicine, of healing the sick, extending lifespans, and allowed people to have children who would otherwise not have been able to. Therefore natural selection, or survival of the fittest does not apply to us, or certainly not in the way we understand it as applying to the rest of the natural world.

Conclusion

As Muslims, our belief is that absolute truth, as described by the Qur'an and authentic Hadith of the Prophet (peace be upon him), and science cannot contradict each other (except in the case of miracles, which are exceptions to Allah's natural laws through His power and permission). Even if something seems contradictory at the moment, it is likely that in the future our understanding of the Qur'an and/or our scientific understanding of the natural world advances and changes in a way that makes sense.

Questions

- What is the theory of evolution?

- What is science?

- Why does Islam promote science?

- What does it mean if science and religion contradict each other?

- Do Muslims believe in the theory of evolution?

Activities

- Do some research regarding Muslim scientists of the past who made great discoveries and advances in their field

- Consider why the Muslim world made such great scientific advances in the past, but is not currently doing so

- Do some research regarding questions and controversies scientists still have about the theory of evolution

Islam, from ancient times to the modern day

1 . 9

Environmentalism

Objectives

- To understand why environmentalism is promoted by Islam

- To explore the impact humans are having on the natural world

- To consider how we, as individuals, can make a difference

Keywords

- Environment

- Stewards

- Creation

- Signs

What effect is human life having on planet Earth?

Human beings are damaging the Earth. To produce energy we are rapidly burning non-renewable fossil fuels (oil, coal, gas) that take millions of years to form. This produces waste such as carbon dioxide gas, which accumulates in our atmosphere and stops the Sun's energy from being able to escape back into space, causing global warming. Gradually, this causes the temperature of the Earth to rise, causing the large amounts of ice at the North and South pole to melt and sea levels to rise, submerging small islands and coastlines. It also disrupts weather patterns all over the world, which leads to floods, hurricanes and tornadoes, heat waves and forest fires.

Pollution from vehicles and industry poison the air and river water, causing breathing illnesses and shortages of clean drinking water. To produce enough meat and food we are cutting down trees and destroying forests to create farmland. Many animals have lost their habitat and hundreds of species have become extinct. We are using pesticides and farming methods that kill pollinating and other helpful insects, causing loss of plant species and slowly eroding the soil, leading to desertification. Animals are farmed in a way to maximise meat, milk, and egg production, which involves feeding them unnatural foods, indoor housing in cramped conditions, and injecting them with drugs and hormones. Overfishing has led to massive reductions in the levels of fish in the oceans, including extinction of many species and disruption of entire ecosystems. Plastic waste has been found in every corner of the world, from the tops of mountains to the ocean floor, in the stomach of dead whales that wash up on beaches and micro-plastics even in the blood of humans.

What can we expect in the future?

If the human population of the world continues to increase and our practices do not change, scientists warn us about what to expect. Loss of pollinating insects will lead to famine, through failure of the agricultural system. Extinction of plant and animal species will be so extreme that entire ecosystems will collapse, on land and in the seas. Increasing pollution will cause widespread illnesses, through breathing of contaminated air and drinking of contaminated water. Sea levels will rise causing coastal villages and cities to be evacuated, and extreme weather patterns will become more frequent. If we take this to its natural conclusion, eventually our planet will become uninhabitable for humans and we will become extinct.

The Divine purpose of creation

What does Islam tell us about how we should treat our environment? As Muslims we believe all of Allah's creation has a purpose. Allah describes humanity as the best of His creation, and tells us that we were created to worship Him, to recognise Him.

We honoured the children of Adam...and favoured them above all Our creation. (Qur'an 17:70)

I created Jinn and human beings only to worship Me. (Qur'an 51:56)

For this purpose, He has created the world around us. In the Qur'an He describes how the rain falls on the earth to allow plants and fruit to grow for us to eat, and how we can use animals for their meat but also milk, and for transport. He describes how ships and the wind allow us to sail across the seas, and how the orbit of the Sun and Moon give us night and day to allow us to work and rest.

For your benefit He created the sea; from it you get fresh meat to eat, and extract jewellery that you wear. You see the ships sailing over the waves to seek His gifts, so you may be thankful. He placed the mountains firmly on the Earth, so it doesn't shake beneath you, made the rivers and the tracks so you can find your way, and many other signposts, including the stars for guiding the travellers. (Qur'an 16:14-16)

In the livestock there is a moral for you; We gave you a drink from

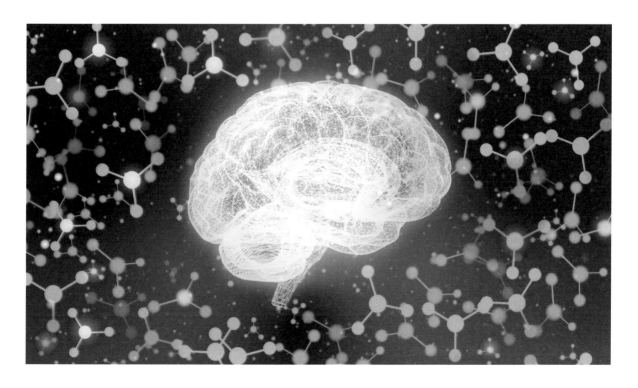

inside their bellies – it is from between the bowels and blood – pure milk, healthy nourishment for its drinkers. And you make juice from the fruits of dates and grapes, delicious and nourishing; in this is a sign for those who understand. Your Lord gave the bee an instinct to build hives in the mountains, the trees and buildings, saying: "Eat the nectar from different fruits and follow the ways of your Lord humbly." Then from its belly comes a syrup of different colours in which there is a healing for people, it is a sign for those who think. (Qur'an 16:66-69)

Allah created the heavens and the Earth and sent down rain from the sky, by which He produced fruits to provide for you, and made possible for you to sail by ship across the sea by His command, made rivers for you, made the sun and the moon, orbiting steadily, and made for you both night and day. (Qur'an 14:32-33)

Allah describes the world as having been created in 'balance', and the natural state of things ('Fitra') is something considered pure and good.

...It is the inclination that God has nurtured the people on. There is no changing in Allah's creation. Such is the pure system... (Qur'an 30:30)

The relationship of a Muslim with their environment

Allah tells us about how our relationship with the rest of His creation should be. In the Qur'an and Hadith we are called representatives of Allah, or stewards of the Earth:

Remember when Your Lord told the Angels: "I am creating a representative on Earth..." (Qur'an 2:30)

"The earth is green and beautiful and Allah has appointed you his stewards over it and He sees how you acquit yourselves." (Muslim)

To understand this let us use an analogy. Imagine you are the chief advisor to a king. The king has given you a position of power and responsibility, the people are under your command, as is the treasury. However, you must remember that the people and the money are not yours even though you have control over them, ultimately they belong to the king. If you were to waste his money and abuse his subjects, this would anger the king and he would punish you. If you spend his money wisely and treat his subjects kindly, the king will be pleased with you and will reward you.

What it means to be a steward

So Allah has blessed us by giving us the ability to shape and change the world around us, to use it to enhance our civilisations. But we must remember that it does not belong to us, ultimately all of creation belongs to the Creator, we are merely its caretakers. Therefore, while using the natural world to fulfil our needs we must treat it with respect and also consider its needs.

In other words, our interaction with our environment needs to be in balance, or sustainable.

This is a way of showing gratitude to Allah, and as He tells us in the Qur'an if we are grateful He will give us even more.

Remember when your Lord declared, "If you are grateful, I will surely increase My favours to you, but if you are ungrateful, then My punishment is severe." (Qur'an 14:7)

If we do not do this, if we treat the natural world as we have been doing this will upset the balance of creation and lead to corruption of the natural state of things, as is already evident in the world around us. This is showing extreme ingratitude and will lead to loss of Allah's blessings in this life and punishment in the next.

If corruption has appeared on land and sea it's because of what people have done with their hands, it is to make them taste something of the fruits of what they have done, so they may turn back from their wicked ways. (Qur'an 30:41)

Recognising and preserving Allah's signs

One of the ways to change our attitude towards the natural world is to gain a greater appreciation of Allah's creation. This is a recurring theme in the Qur'an, we are repeatedly told to look at the world around us, at the heavens and the stars, at mountains and oceans, animals and plants, to consider how intricate and marvellous their creation is. When we take the time to observe and study them, this will reveal the majesty of the Creator and bring us closer to Allah. Everything that Allah has created is a sign that leads back to him, and so it is our duty to honour and preserve these signs, to gain guidance ourselves but also for future generations to be able to benefit. Apart from the spiritual, this also has a physical manifestation. Many of the advances humanity have made in science have come from studying the natural world, including medicines such as antibiotics.

In the creation of the Heavens and the Earth, in the cycle of night and day, and in the ships which sail the seas for the people's profit; in the rain Allah sends down from the skies, bringing the dead earth to life, and causing it to abound with all kinds of animals; in the movements of the winds, and in the clouds which float between Heaven and Earth: in all these things, there are signs for people who understand. (Qur'an 2:164)

In the creation of the Heavens and the Earth and the cycle of night and day, there are signs for people of understanding, who remember Allah standing, sitting and lying down, and think about the creation of the Heavens and the Earth, prayerfully saying, "Our Lord, You haven't created this in vain..." (Qur'an 3:190-191)

Having love and respect for all of Allah's creation

Even though animals do not have the same level of consciousness as humans, Allah has created them with emotions, they can feel fear and pain, happiness and love.

There is no creature on land or a bird flying in the sky that does not belong to a community just like yours... (Qur'an 6:38)

There were many instances in the life of the Prophet (peace be upon him) when he showed kindness to animals and advised his companions to do the same, admonishing people who treated them callously or without thought to their physical and emotional welfare. He told us how an act of kindness to an animal can be enough for Allah to grant a person Paradise, and conversely how cruelty to animals can lead to Hell.

The Prophet (peace be upon him) said, "A woman was punished due to a cat she had imprisoned until it died, so she entered the Hellfire. She did not give it food or water while it was imprisoned, neither did she set it free to eat from the vermin of the earth." (Bukhari)

Furthermore, the Qur'an also tells us that all of Allah's creation, even things we consider as inanimate and lifeless (such as rocks), are constantly engaged in the worship of Allah in ways we cannot hear, recognise or even imagine:

The seven Heavens and the Earth and what is in them all glorify Him; there isn't a single thing that doesn't glorify and praise Him, but you don't understand their way of celebrating His glory... (Qur'an 17:44)

Haven't you considered, everything in the Heavens and the Earth glorifies Allah? The birds flying in flocks, each one knows how it should pray and glorify Him; and Allah knows what they do. (Qur'an 24:41)

The above Qur'anic verses indicate to us that Allah's creation is interwoven and interdependent, the biological concept of ecosystem, in which animals and plants interact to survive. We need to recognise that we are a part of this world, we cannot survive without it, and so part of our worship of Allah is to act in accordance with these principles.

This also touches upon other Islamic principles, such as helping

those less fortunate than ourselves. The effects of pollution and climate change disproportionately affect the poorest people in the world, making their lives even more difficult through loss of homes and livelihood, disease and death. These are the very people Allah and His Prophet (peace be upon him) encourage us to look after, who we are told have a right upon our wealth.

...the worshippers, who perform their prayer constantly, in whose wealth is a due share for the beggar and the deprived... (Qur'an 70:24-25)

How can we make a difference?

On an individual level what does this mean? How can we change our practice to treat the environment in accordance with Islamic principles? It is unlikely most of us are in a position to enact large projects, such as the setting up of wildlife parks and nature reserves. However, if we were, this is a practice of the Prophet (peace be upon him) called 'Hima'. During his lifetime he set up an area to the south of Madina where hunting was forbidden within a four-mile radius and destruction of trees or plants was forbidden within a twelve mile radius.

Islamic countries, especially of the Middle East, should invest in renewable energy sources such as solar, and wherever new Mosques are being built they should be designed to be carbon neutral (see example of new Cambridge Central Mosque). As individual Muslims we should be supportive of national and international projects to reduce the negative impact we are having on the planet and move towards sustainability. This should be a factor in who we vote for at a local and national level.

Within our families we should encourage learning about the world around us. This includes experiencing it directly by visiting local nature reserves and parks, and when we go on holiday to explore amazing natural phenomenon in different parts of the world. We should read books and watch nature documentaries. This is what the Qur'an is telling us to do, to ponder the signs and creation of Allah, to consider how amazing the Creator of all of this must be.

We should take part in activities to reduce our carbon footprint and help the environment. This includes reducing the use of our cars, instead walking or cycling whenever we can, or using public transport. When we are deciding on what kind of car to buy, we should take into consideration its fuel consumption and the amount of pollution it produces.

Islam, from ancient times to the modern day

We should plant trees and look after a garden. The Prophet (peace be upon him) told us this is an act of continuing charity, which we can benefit from even after we die. Whenever any person or animal gains benefit from what we have planted and taken care of, Allah will reward us.

The Prophet (peace be upon him) said: "If a Muslim plants a tree or sows seeds, and then a bird, or a person or an animal eats from it, it is regarded as a charitable gift (Sadaqah) for him." (Bukhari)

The Prophet (peace be upon him) said: "If the Hour (the day of Resurrection) is about to be established and one of you was holding a palm shoot, let him take advantage of even one second before the Hour is established to plant it." (Al Albani)

This also includes reducing waste. Allah forbids us from being wasteful in the Qur'an, clearly stating that He does not like those who waste.

...and do not squander; He dislikes spendthrifts. (Qur'an 6:141)

The Prophet (peace be upon him) happened to pass by a companion, Sa'd (may Allah be pleased with him), as he was performing ablution (Wudu) next to a river. At this, the Prophet said, "Sa'd what is this squandering?" Sa'd replied: "Can there be an idea of squandering (israf) in ablution?" The Prophet (peace be upon him)

said: "Yes, even if you are by the side of a flowing river." (Ibn Majah)

So we should be careful of the amount of food and clothes we end up throwing away, instead buying and consuming less in the first place, or at least giving to charity, the homeless or recycling whatever we can. The Prophet (peace be upon him) used to mend his own shoes:

Syedatuna Aisha (may Allah be pleased with her) was asked: "What did the Messenger of Allah (peace be upon him) do in his house?" She said: "He used to stitch his garment, mend his shoes and work as other men work in their houses." (Ahmad)

We should reduce the amount of meat we eat, since the meat industry has a hugely negative impact on the environment and their treatment

of animals is most often not in keeping with Islamic principles. We should remember that the Prophet (peace be upon him) had a mainly vegetarian diet, which would also be of benefit to our health. The food we buy, including milk and eggs, fruit and vegetables, should be free-range and organic, even if this costs a little extra.

When we are giving money in charity to help those around the world less fortunate than ourselves, we can allocate a share of that money towards projects that benefit people through helping the environment. This could include the digging of wells, or planting of olive trees.

Conclusion

Environmentalism is a fundamental part of Islam, as we believe that all of Allah's creation has value and purpose. It is our duty, as the pinnacle of that creation to derive benefit from but also protect it. With Allah's blessing comes responsibility. Through striving to fulfil our responsibility and maintain harmony and balance, we will be helping the natural world, through which we are ultimately helping ourselves, both physically and spiritually. We should not become disheartened with the state of the natural world we see around us today through centuries of waste, neglect and destruction. Nor should we consider ourselves helpless as a single person with no power or influence. As Muslims, we should always strive to do what is morally right as per Allah's command and the Prophet's example (peace be upon him), and to advise others within our sphere of influence to do the same. If everyone was to make an effort, with the help of Allah, nothing is impossible.

Questions

- What are the effects of human activity on planet Earth?

- If humanity was to continue on its current course, what results would this have?

- As a Muslim, how do we believe Allah has blessed humanity through the natural world?

- What relationship should a Muslim have with their environment?

- How can we help protect the environment, on a small and large scale?

Activities

- Watch a documentary about human impact on global warming and climate change

- Watch a documentary about human activity on forests and animals in different parts of the world

- Plant a tree and/or tend to a garden and try to grow some fruit and vegetables

- Reduce the amount of time you spend in a car, instead using public transport, cycling or walking

- Reduce the amount of things you throw away, including food, old possessions and clothes; instead give to charities and try to recycle more

- Find out about initiatives in your neighbourhood or city to help the environment, and get involved

Glossary

Ablution / Wudu – the act of washing ourselves or part of our body, a type of ritual purification

Adhan – the Islamic call to prayer

Ahl al-Bayt – people of the house, refers to family of the Prophet Muhammad (peace be upon him)

Al-Lawh al-Mahfuz – the Preserved Tablet, upon which is inscribed everything that has, and will ever happen

Awliyah Allah – friends of Allah, the saints

Barakat – blessings

Dawah – invitation to Islam

Fard – obligatory

Fiqh – Islamic jurisprudence, i.e., the science of deriving and understanding Shariah, or Islamic law

Fitra – a state of purity and innocence that all human beings are born with, our innate nature

Ghusl – a type of ritual purification that involves washing our whole body

Hadith – a record of the words or actions of the Prophet Muhammad (peace be upon him)

Hadith Kudsi – a Hadith in which the content is directly revealed by Allah, but the wording is attributed to the Prophet Muhammad (peace be upon him)

Hajj / Umrah – the greater and lesser pilgrimage to Makkah, one of the five pillars of Islam

Halal – permissible

Haram – impermissible

Hijab – a religious veil worn by women, usually covering the head and chest

Hafiz / Hafiza / Huffaz – the masculine, feminine and plural form of the word denoting someone who has memorised the entire Qur'an

Ihsan – beautification, perfection, or excellence

Istighfar – repentance, seeking forgiveness

Jihad – to struggle or strive

Jinn – the only other creation of Allah other than humans to have free will. They were created from a smokeless fire, and are invisible to humans but can appear in different forms

Madhab – a school of religious law

Mus'haf – the written form of the Qur'an

Nafs – has been defined in various ways, including the self, the soul, the ego, the psyche

Nawafil – voluntary or supererogatory acts of worship

Qadr – predestination, the Divine will

Rak'at – a single unit of prayer in the Salah

Riba – usury / interest, or any other form of exploitation or unjust gain made in trade or business

Sadaqa / Zakat – voluntary and obligatory charity, one of the five pillars of Islam

Salah – ritual prayers performed by Muslims while facing the direction of the Ka'ba, alone or in congregation, including the five obligatory daily prayers which are one of the five pillars of Islam

Sawm – fasting, obligatory within the month of Ramadan, or voluntary fasting at any other time of the year, one of the five pillars of Islam

Shai'tan/Iblis – Satan / the devil, a Jinn who lived with the Angels in the Heavens prior to disobeying Allah

Shariah – Islamic law

Siratul Mustaqim – the straight path, the middle way (i.e., in between extremes)

Sunnah – traditions and practices of the Prophet Muhammad (peace be upon him) which provide a model for how Muslims should live their lives

Syedina / Syedatuna – masculine and feminine form of a term used as a title or out of respect, meaning 'our leader' or 'our master'

Taqwa – consciousness of Allah that stops us from disobeying Him in fear of His anger and punishment

Tassawuf / Sufism – the facet of Islam concerned with purification of the inner and outer self

Tawakkul – trust / reliance in Allah

Ummah – a people, community or nation, used in the Qur'an to denote the people to whom Allah sends a Prophet (peace be upon them all)

Zina – fornication or adultery